A GIFT
OF
L♥VE &
LAUGHTER

TO: _____

FROM: _____

BOOK DESCRIPTION

On the OUTSIDE... It's uniquely designed with the look of an already gift-wrapped present.

On the INSIDE... It's two hundred fun-filled, jam-packed pages of wit, whimsy and heart-felt funniness.

It's an easy, joyful read.

It's a feel-good collection of *silly short stories, playful poetry, quirky quotes, and comical cartoons.* It offers inspiring thoughts and themes of hopes and dreams, and lots and lots of love and laughter. It's written with the intent that each word is worth a thousand pictures.

It's created to be a great gift for someone special in your life... For *Christmas, Birthdays, Anniversaries, Valentine's Day, Mother's Day, Father's Day, as a Thank You, Bon Voyage, or Get-Well gift ... Or just because you care!*

It's hoped that this book will make hearts smile, both when it's given and when it's received.

I hope this book makes your heart smile.

Love to all,

Ron SEVERINI

A GIFT
OF
LOVE & LAUGHTER

Words and Musings
Ron SEVERINI

© Copyright 2022 / The SEVERINI Company, LLC
ALL RIGHTS RESERVED

No portion of this book may be reproduced, distributed, or transmitted in any form, by any means, including photocopying, recording, scanning, etc. or by any other means whatsoever, including, but not limited, to electronic, photographic, or mechanical methods, nor may it be stored in any retrieval system, transmitted, or otherwise copied for public or private use without the prior written, signed and dated permission of the publisher.

It is illegal to copy or distribute any portion of this book without written, signed, and dated permission of the publisher.

PUBLISHER

The SEVERINI Company, LLC
P.O. BOX 3187
Windermere, FL 34786
info@TheSEVERINICompany.com

Book Design: Ron SEVERINI
Cover Concept: Ron SEVERINI
Photography: Ron SEVERINI
Book Editor: Carol Skuratofsky
Cover Design: Leslie Ann Akin
Image Editor: Leslie Ann Akin
Printing: Digital Publishing

Paperback ISBN: 978-1-7340448-3-6
E-Book ISBN: 978-1-7340448-4-3
Hard Cover ISBN: 978-1-7340448-5-0
Library of Congress Control Number: 2022921559

OFFICIAL FIRST EDITION: 11/29/2022

The SEVERINI COMPANY, LLC

www.TheSEVERINIcompany.com

The SEVERINI Company, LLC is a privately held corporation headquartered in Windermere (Orlando) Florida. Our mission is to dream, create and offer for sale unique treasures for "children of all ages".

These creations include books, gifts, novelty items, screen plays, live shows, TV shows and indie movies. Products include anything that the imagination of The SEVERINI Company, LLC can dream up and create, as long as it's unique, fun and can bring a smile to the heart of those that experience them.

DEDICATION

This book is dedicated
to the three most important females in my life.

To MARY - My Mother
You gave me life. You gave me unconditional love.
Your unwavering belief in me was unparalleled.
To always trust my gut instinct was incalculable advice.
To always follow my dreams was my life's roadmap.
I can still hear your angelic voice, counseling me:
"When one door closes, another shall open."
I loved you mom, and I shall love you forever and a day.
I dedicate this book to you.

To CAROL
You are a miracle muse.
You made this book be all it could be ... and more.
I dedicate this book to you.

To ANNIE - My Grand Daughter
To the one-of-a kind, amazingly, gifted little girl that calls me
Pop-Pop and melts me.
The day you were born was the day God sent down from
heaven his most precious angel, posing as a beautiful child.
There is nothing I will not do for you.
I love you Annie, and I shall love you forever and a day.
I dedicate this book to you.

DISCLAIMER

In certain instances, within this book, various names, characters, businesses, places, events, incidents, etc. may be the product of the author's creativity or imagination or may have been used in an alternate or fictitious manner; thus, any resemblance to actual persons, living or dead, or actual events, may be purely coincidental.

In certain instances, the author may have witnessed or experienced certain details differently than others, especially due to the author's unique vantage point or memory. In certain instances, the author may have taken artistic license to embellish certain details, stories, or information for comedic or dramatic effect. In certain instances, the author may have offered tribute to a celebrity, act, artist, etc. In certain instances, comments, quotes, sayings, etc. may seem similar to others' thoughts, quotes, sayings, etc. but these are certainly only purely coincidental. The author makes no representations or warranties expressed or implied, about the completeness, accuracy, reliability, suitability, or availability with respect to the information contained for any purpose. Any unauthorized use of any contents is strictly prohibited.

The author assumes no responsibility for errors, inaccuracies, omissions, inconsistencies, and hereby disclaims any liability to any party for any loss, damage, disruption, etc. caused by errors or omissions, whether such errors or omissions result from negligence, accident, or any other cause. The author makes no guarantee concerning the level of success anyone may attain or experience by following any thought, advice, idea, testimonial, example, strategy, quote, saying contained etc. as they may not apply to any reader, thus are not intended to guarantee anyone will achieve any positive or specific result.

To the maximum extent permitted by law, the author disclaims all liability in the event anything contained within proves to be inaccurate, incomplete, unreliable, etc. or results in any damage, loss, or negative result. The author disclaims all liability in connection with the use of any of the information written, drawn, inferred, provided, or included, which is included solely for entertainment purposes only.

A Gift of Love & Laughter

LIST OF LISTS

I'm the kind of person people refer to as a "List maker."
I make and keep a list of almost everything in my life.

I have a list of ...

Groceries TO BUY
Things TO DO
Things TO FIX
Items TO PURCHASE
Ideas TO DEVELOP
Inventions TO MAKE
Poems, Short Stories and Screenplays TO WRITE
Books TO READ
Gifts TO SEND
Things that make me HAPPY
Things for which I am THANKFUL
People that have PURCHASED MY BOOKS
Favorite QUOTES
Favorite SONGS
CITIES I have VISITED
PLACES I would like TO VISIT
MOVIES and LIVE SHOWS I have VIEWED
LAKES where I'd like to go trout fishing
BLOOD PRESSURE and HEART RATE levels
And certainly, I have a BUCKET LIST
And now I have this LIST OF LISTS

HOWEVER, the list YOU might like most, is the following *LIST OF CONTENTS* within this book...

LIST OF CONTENTS

DEDICATION	ix
DISCLAIMER	x
LIST OF LISTS	xiii
A WISE OLD PHYSICIAN ONCE SAID	xvii
TODAY	2
PERFECT	3
FUN WORDS	6
KID IN A CANDY STORE	10
I'M A BOOMER BABY	17
THE SUMMER OF LOVE	19
IT'S ABOUT TIME	38
CANNOLIS	42
TIME	43
LIFE IS SHORT	44
TWENTIETH CENTURY SLANG	45
A TWENTIETH CENTURY SLANG POEM	48
YOU CAN'T GO BACK	50
DOWN THE SHORE	52
DREAMS	53
SLEEP	55
FOLLOW YOUR DREAMS	57
MY DREAM	58
The MIGHTY OAK	60
PLAN "A"	61
PLAN "BE"	62
IT'S NEVER TOO LATE	63
MAKE 'EM LAUGH	66
LAUGHTER	68
CIRCLE THE WORDS	69
HAVE A NICE DAY	71

LOVE QUOTES	78
TRUE LOVE IS	79
I'D CHOOSE YOU	80
EQUATIONS OF L♥VE	82
HOW SHALL I EXPRESS MY LOVE TO YOU?	83
ALL I NEED IS YOU	84
THE GREATEST THING YOU'LL EVER LEARN	85
We LIVED We LAUGHED We LOVED	86
A QUIET PLACE	88
LOVE	90
TO ALL THE CHILDREN OF THE WORLD	92
AN OLD IRISH BLESSING	94
KID TOYS	95
PLAY BALL	99
MAKE A PURE WISH	101
INSPIRATION	103
FRIENDSHIP	105
BEFORE	108
CHOOSE	109
IT'S YOUR ROAD	112
MOMENTS FOR ME	113
DESTINY	114
FORGIVENESS	115
WORDS OF WISDOM	117
SHIFTING	118
HAPPY ME	119
THE VAULT	121
THE PRETZEL LADY AND THE STOCKBROKER	123
THE GOLDFISH BOWL	125
YOUR SMILE	128
FRECKLES	129
A GOLF STORY	131
A SIMPLE LIFE	133
FOR THOSE THAT THINK	136

THE LITTLE BOWL	137
IS IT TRUE?	139
THE DRAWINGS	140
SILLY STORIES	149
TOMMY THE TURKEY BOY	152
LOONEY LARRY	153
THE QUIRKY CHEMIST	155
The FISHERMAN and the RABBI	157
FICTIONAL CHARACTERS	161
I BELIEVE	162
A FULL GLASS OF LIFE	167
FULL	171
BE THANKFUL	175
THANK YOU	176
ABOUT THE AUTHOR	177

A WISE OLD PHYSICIAN ONCE SAID

"The best medicine for humans is

LOVE and LAUGHTER."

Someone asked:

"What if it doesn't work?"

He smiled and answered:

"Increase the dose!"

Sunrise over LAKE BUTLER

Windermere, Florida

TODAY

TODAY, I'm going to be happy.
TODAY, I'm going to be nice.
If anyone tries to ruin my day,
I'll just have to read this twice.

PERFECT

This story is about the word PERFECT.

Actually, the word PERFECT is my favorite word of all the words in the English language.

To me, no word can be more PERFECT than the word PERFECT.

Just the mere sound of the word PERFECT is PERFECT to me.

Whenever I hear the word PERFECT, I start to feel better. I feel whole. It makes me feel like I've attained the ultimate goal I was aiming for or I've completed a task flawlessly or found exactly what I was looking for.

I know it is said, *"Nothing is PERFECT,"* but I beg to differ, and I refuse to believe it. I shall explain ...

It is my contention that there IS such a thing as PERFECT because PERFECT can be achieved. For example, when I was a young boy taking music lessons, my guitar teacher always assured me: *"Practice makes PERFECT!"* So there, PERFECT can be achieved ... all you need to do is practice, practice, practice! ☺

I know that explanation may sound like a bit of a stretch but stick with me and follow along as I seriously explain in PERFECT detail why the word PERFECT is the ultimate and PERFECT word of all words.

First, let's dissect the word PERFECT. PERFECT comes from the Latin word: *perficere* which breaks down into per (completely) and facere (do).

Next, the grammar books tell us the word PERFECT can be an adjective or a verb.

As an adjective: *"He has drawn a PERFECT circle."*

As a verb: *"The Olympic gold-medal winner PERFECTED his acrobatic routine after many years of practice."*

The dictionary explains PERFECT in this manner: *"Something that is PERFECT is something that is entirely without fault, without defect or without blemish, something that satisfies all requirements, something that is precisely accurate, exact, excellent, or complete."*

PERFECT is something that conforms to a description or definition of an ideal type as in a *perfect* sphere, or he was a *perfect* gentleman.

Here are sentences that include the word PERFECT:

"It was a PERFECT day!"

"That was the PERFECT answer."

"In baseball a no hitter is a PERFECT game."

"A flawless diamond is PERFECT."

"That bottle of Merlot was the PERFECT wine with that pasta."

Those individuals that aim for something to always be PERFECT are referred to as PERFECTIONISTS.

A *Perfectionist is: "Someone with very high standards, or someone that wants everything to be just right at all times."*

To be honest, I have been told by many friends and family members that I am a PERFECTIONIST. I humbly feel they are PERFECT in their assessment.

I do not agree with those nay-sayers that spout a blanket statement that *"Nothing is PERFECT."* If those nay-sayers are correct and *"Nothing is PERFECT"* and PERFECT doesn't exist, then it seems funny to me that there are so many words that PERFECTLY describe something that is PERFECT such as:

Flawless; Faultless; Seamless; Spotless; Unblemished; Undamaged; Unmarred; Unimpaired; Unspoiled; Untarnished; Unbroken; Consummate; Ultimate; Supreme; Mint: Optimal; Complete; Incomparable; Unequaled; Unmatched; Unrivaled; Unsurpassable; Peerless; Pure

So, there you have it ... PERFECT does exist.

However, if you still feel that nothing is PERFECT, then I shall leave you with this final thought ... "if nothing is PERFECT then PERFECT is nothing ... and there's no sense in me writing any more about 'nothing' ... so, if you still feel that I have not fully explained the word PERFECT, then please forgive me ... nobody's PERFECT!"

FUN WORDS

There's a plethora of fun words in the English language that I find playful and amusing. Whether you're a wisenheimer, a young whippersnapper or an old fuddy-duddy, these words may sound like gibberish, gobbledygook or mumbo-jumbo. Let's peruse a smattering and have some fun. Maybe you'll even find a few to add to your own vocabulary.

To begin, I love ONOMATOPOEIA. The dictionary defines ONOMATOPEIA as *"A word or figure of speech in which words evoke the actual sound of the thing they describe."*

For example, there are clock related onomatopoeia words like cuckoo, boing, tick-tock and dingdong. There are machine related onomatopoeia words that describe noises like bing, bang, boom, cling, clang, click, clunk, crash, crackle, crunch, and of course, clickety-clack and clip-petty-clop. There are also onomatopoeia animal noises such as bark, meow, moo, oink, roar, growl, quack, snarl, gobble, cackle, croak, cheep, chirp, caw, coo, squawk, hiss, warble, woof and whinny. .

Next, the following are not necessarily onomatopoeia words but still have a fun sound to them. These words fall in the human noise making category such as burp, blab and blurt, as well as hush, hum, hiccup, moan, mumble, murmur, chuckle, whine, whisper, eek, clap, sob, squeal, yawn, boohoo, munch, mutter, shush, slurp, gulp, guzzle, gasp, gobble, groan, gag, glug, grunt, and grumble ... and don't forget giggle, gaggle and gargle.

And wait.... there's more ...
There's bam, bang, boom, bash, bubble, blubber, click, clank, clink, clash, creak, clatter, fizz, fizzle, flick, flack, flip, flutter, pop, plop, poof, pow, puff, ooze, ring, rattle, rustle, kaboom and kerplunk.

And lest we not forget ... slurp, slop, spit, sputter, snip, and snap, split and splat, splish and splash, squish and squelch, sizzle, and swizzle, as well as skedaddle, thud, thump, thwack, tinkle, trickle, wallop, whack, wham, whiz, whoop, whoosh, vroom, zip, zap and the ever-popular trio of zing zang and zoom.

There it is, that's all she wrote, lickety-split, I'm done for now. I can't dilly dally ... times up for any rigamarole, malarky, poppycock, hanky-panky, hogwash, lollygagging, wishy-washy hoo-hah, folderol, or any type of bombastic or silly shenanigans.

I hope you have not felt bamboozled, hoodwinked, ramshackled, molly-coddled or discombobulated. I've given you the absolute best of my bailey-wick, including the whole enchilada, the kitchen sink, the entire megillah, and certainly, the kitten-caboodle.

So ... please, go get some type of whirly-gig, doohickey, thingamajig or whatchamacallit to help you save these precious fun words. Put them in a cubbyhole, store them in noodle or noggin, and insert them into your next conversation; all will be hunky-dory especially if your conversation is with a bimbo, bozo, buffoon, nincompoop, namby-pamby, hotsy-totsy, hoity toity, ragamuffin or scallywag. Don't be wishy-washy or a party-pooper about it all, and there's certainly, no need to get flabbergasted.

So, I'm counting on everyone reading this to use and share these particularly peculiar, aberrant adjectives with all your busybody, long-winded, chatterbox, dingleberry friends, especially if you're an overly verbose, deep-throated, lose-lipped, flap-jawing, canary-like, gossip-spreading, blow-hard blabbermouth.

Tah Tah

OUR CANDY STORE
ORANGE AVENUE & MADISON AVENUE
IRVINGTON, NJ

KID IN A CANDY STORE

It has always made me laugh out loud (LOL) whenever someone would banter the phrase: *"Like a kid in a candy store"*. You see, I was born in the back room of my parent's little, corner, candy store in Irvington, NJ in the late 1940's. That's where I spent the first eighteen years of my life. I was told my first toy was an empty Coca Cola bottle. That doesn't surprise me because in addition to soda pop, we sold one-cent Bazooka Joe bubble gum, five-cent Topps baseball cards, packs of Juicy Fruit gum, Hershey chocolate bars, candy apples and cups of homemade, Italian lemon ice. I could eat or drink anything I wanted, but by the time I was nine, I had had my fill of chocolate ... especially Chunky Bars (which were my favorite of all the candies). You'd think the concept of eating whatever you wanted, (especially sugar-sweet candy) whenever you wanted, would be an amazing experience for a kid. Well, it was for a while, but soon after nine years of age it didn't have the same appeal it once had held.

I heard a similar story from a friend that ran the roller coaster ride at our neighborhood amusement park, Olympic Park. He could ride that roller coaster whenever he wanted, but by his third day on the job he said, *"the thrill was gone"*. Just too much of a good thing.

During the holidays we sold Christmas trees outside our candy store. We ordered one thousand trees each season, and our family could have had the pick-of-the-litter if we had wanted. (Well, not really - no we couldn't.) We always sold the best trees to make the most money. We could then pick our family tree to go into our living room from the remaining left-over trees.

Same thing happened when we added a deli case and sold cold cuts. My father had a saying, *"We sell the best and eat the rest."* So, when we wanted to make a sandwich for ourselves, we had to go to the bottom of the deli tray and slice up from the left-over end pieces. (It was all okay since we did have a choice whether we wanted ham, turkey, or bologna; the only rule was we had to make our sandwich from the "heel" part of the left-over meats.)

Since we also branched out and sold groceries, and since I was the oldest, I was appointed the official "delivery boy." By nine years old, along with my trusty little red wagon, I delivered bags and bags of groceries to all our customers that were the "shut-ins" of the neighborhood (nice people, all of them). This gave me an opportunity to learn about all types of people. I learned there was a unique story within each one of those houses.

So, at age nine, I started to work. Unfortunately, I had needed to leave the playground early in order to do my deliveries, therefore I couldn't finish playing stickball on those days with my buddies. I learned in life that *"you gotta do what you gotta do,"* and this was what I needed to do for the family business, so I did it. My father always told me that *"we work for pennies and eventually they'll turn into dollars."*

A Gift of Love & Laughter

Anyway, I'll tell you about a couple of those customers ...

First, was Orange Ave. Living all alone, was a little old lady whom I'll refer to as Mrs. S. She was at least ninety years old with stark, white hair that looked identical to the white, cotton tops in a Q-tip box. Mrs. S. would call our store and order about twenty dollars' worth of groceries to be delivered. (Campbells chicken noodle soup, Chef Boy-R-Dee spaghetti in a can, Jiff peanut butter, Welch's grape jelly, a brand-new loaf of Wonder Bread, lots of Maxwell House coffee cans, a five-pound heavy bag of sugar and a big ten-pound box of Tide laundry detergent.) This was a big order back in the 1950s. That order filled up four brown paper sack bags, and an order that size would probably cost about one hundred and fifty dollars now.

Mrs. S. lived a mile away and the pre-war, grey slate sidewalks, were bumpy due to very old, oak tree roots protruding through the ground. I had to go very slow with my wagon. When I finally arrived at her house, I rolled my little red wagon up her front yard walkway. Next, I had to take one bag at a time, climb up her steep, Victorian front steps, and one by one, go through the wide, wooden, front porch, through and past the twelve-foot tall, stained-glass mahogany front door, through her front living room (which she called the parlor) and finally into her dining room. She would never allow me into her kitchen because she had a big, thick, dark, hand-sewn patchwork blanket hanging between the kitchen and the dining room.

Now, Mrs. S. couldn't hear well, so I always had to repeat myself or yell loudly. Anyway, what was always so strange was that every time I delivered her groceries, I saw about eight clothes lines stretched across her living room, above her head height and hanging on each of those clothes lines were $10 and $20-dollar bills held on by old, wooden, clothes pins (brand new, crisp, washed and ironed $10s and $20s all in a row!) There had to have been a thousand dollars' worth. I thought she was either a counter-fitter or a clean freak, or maybe someone once told her to "watch" her money, and she thought they said to "wash" her money.

Mrs. S. always smiled and just kept smiling all the time - happiest old lady I ever met. When I finally got done with the entire project of pulling my wagon for a mile, and carrying ALL those bags of groceries one by one, up all those stairs, and parking them all on her huge, dining room table, she'd stop, tell me to close my eyes, and then she'd bend over and kiss me on my cheek, proudly announce: *"guess what I have for you? .... A shiny new dime."* A dime. She had $1,000 dollars hanging on a clothesline, and she gives me a *shiny* new dime as if she was giving me the Hope Diamond!

Well, my father always told me to keep a happy grin on my face, and always be nice to the customers. So, that's what I did. I pretended like she was the most generous person in the world. I smiled, and said, *"OH, Thank You Mrs. S. ... have a nice day ... and ... THANK YOU for shopping at our store."*
I'd walk out of her dining room, through the living room, across the front porch, down those steep steps, grab my little, red wagon, and walk a mile back to our store; however, this time, I walked back a much richer kid because I had *a shiny new dime* in my pocket.

I'd always go back to our store and tell my father about the bills hanging from the clothesline, and I'd always show him my *shiny* new dime. And he'd always smile and tell me, *"You know, after ten trips to Mrs. S's house, you'll eventually have a dollar, and someday, when you get ten of those dollars in your jar, you too can have a $10 bill hanging on a cloth line if you want."* I didn't really know what to make of that fatherly advice back then, but I did put my *shiny new dime* in my tip jar under my bed, and those dimes did eventually add up to dollars.   Took a while. Oh, the benefits of being "a kid in a candy store."

Next was Cummings Street. Never knew her name ... a nice young lady ... lived alone ... kind of pretty, but never smiled ... maybe thirty years old. Her house was only a couple of blocks from our store. Once a week she would order a couple bags of groceries, along with two, six-packs of coca cola.

What was unique about the Cummings Street house was that she only had one arm - just her left arm. Each time I arrived at her house; I'd hear the most wonderful piano music coming from inside. When I rang her bell, the music would immediately stop; she'd come to the front door; open it, but would stand sideways, always keeping her left side toward me. Each time I'd carry in another bag, she'd pivot, and turn to face me as I was coming in, so as never to allow me to ever see her right side (missing arm). I knew she was extremely self-conscious about it; she must have been hiding in her house for years so nobody could see her; so sad to me.

It was always the same ritual. I'd carry in the two or three bags of groceries (milk, eggs, bread, honey, oatmeal, raisins, two six-packs of coca cola, and lots of Campbell chicken noodle soup) and put them on her kitchen table. She had no furniture in her living room which was odd – just a big, white, baby grand piano. Of course, I thought to myself, *'how does a one-armed person play the piano,'* but she did. I know she did. I always heard her playing just before I'd ring her bell.

When I finished carrying her groceries into her kitchen, she would always have two, empty, six-packs of coke bottles waiting for me to return. Back in those days each small, empty soda bottle was worth two cents in return; thus, those twelve empties were worth twenty-four cents. (That would be my tip – twenty-four cents in returned empty coke bottles.) I'd have to settle with my father when I returned to the store.

She'd always had a big, fat, hot, homemade, oatmeal raisin cookie waiting for me on a plate, atop a pure, white, cotton handkerchief. I would always grab that cookie and take a great big bite right there in front of her so she could see me enjoying it. It was the only time she ever smiled. Then she would always ask me the same question: *"So, how are those big, wonderful, five cent salty pretzels that your dad sells in the store?"* And I'd always respond, *"They are delicious."* And she'd say, *"I think I'll have to order one for myself someday"*. Then, I'd finish my cookie, wipe off my mouth with the handkerchief, and we would both say goodbye.

Then she would close and double bolt the lock on her front door. I wouldn't depart right away; instead, I'd sit on her front step for a bit and listen to the most amazing piano music coming from inside her house. She'd always play the same song and happily sing, *"Put on a Happy Face"*. I knew she knew I was listening outside. When the song was over, I would make my way back to my dad's store with those twelve, clinking, empty coke bottles, with a smile on my face, my tummy filled with a hot, homemade, oatmeal raisin cookie ... and the knowledge that I had put one of those big, fat, salty pretzels in her bag as a special treat, free of charge. Good memories being *a kid in a candy store.*

I'M A BOOMER BABY

(People born between 1946 – 1964)

Jerry Mathers, Eddie Haskell,
Spanky and the Little Rascals,

Mr. Ed, Dennis the Menace,
Jonathan Winters, Jose Jimenez,

Gene Autry, Roy Rogers,
The Milwaukee Braves, The Brooklyn Dodgers,

Sonny & Cher, Elvis, Dion,
American Bandstand, I wanted to be on,

The Topps, The Temps, The Byrds, The Stones,
Five Cent Candies, Ten Cent Phones,

Bobby & Sissy, Betty Boop,
Duncan Yo-Yo's, Hula Hoops,

Mighty Mouse, Pepe' Le Pew,
Rocky & Bullwinkle, to name a few,

Judy Garland, Mickey Rooney,
George's Aunt, Rose Mary Clooney,

"Here comes da Judge", "There goes my Baby",
Milton Berle, dressed like a Lady,

Do the Twist, the Hop, the Monkey,
Any hip beat to make a white guy funky,

It's Cool, it's Boss, I dig it, it's Groovy,
I'm Mod, I'm Hip, so Sock It To Me!

One step for Mankind, Two for the show,
3-D Glasses, Go Man Go!

Jackson Five, Sixteen Candles,
Number Seven, Mickey Mantle,

Fathers Knows Best, Zappa and the Mothers,
The Lennon Sisters, Dr Joyce Brothers,

Tom Terrific, Lost in Space,
Soupy Sales throws a pie in your face,

Ben Casey, Dr. Kildare,
Brylcreem will give you a full head of hair,

George Jetson, Fred Flintstone,
Kookie, Kookie, lend me your comb.

Green stamps, One red cent,
You'll wonder where the yellow went,

Queen for a Day, "Friday night Fights"
Ripped Levis and cool black lights,

Nothing cooler, it ain't no rumor
I'm proud to be a Baby Boomer!

THE SUMMER OF LOVE

... and what a summer it was!

1969 was a good year to be a nineteen-year-old hippy in America. Like many of my closest friends, I was a musician. My instrument of choice was bass guitar. I always loved music. Back then, I loved oldies, rock 'n roll, pop, folk, country, jazz, blues and even Gershwin. Here's how I spent my time during "The summer of 1969" ...

FILMORE EAST - The music "scene" in America was evolving rapidly throughout the sixties, becoming more diverse and mature than the rock 'n roll of the fifties. At one time, as a young teenage music lover, I was only able to enjoy listening to my favorite artists on a 45 or 33 LP record or view them on TV. As an older teenager, I could attend live performances in medium to large-sized nightclubs and make-shift, movie theaters. Also, now there were even top-named recording acts booked at larger civic centers and auditoriums. New York City's Fillmore East on Second Avenue & Sixth Street, near St Marks Place in Greenwich Village was the hippest and "grooviest" venue around. Getting to "The Fillmore" from my home was a sixty-five-cent bus ride to the Port Authority in midtown Manhattan, followed by a subway ride to the east village.

The FILLMORE EAST

Bill Graham, owner of the Fillmore East (originally built as a Yiddish Theater, now turned concert hall) and the Filmore West, in San Francisco, was also the booking agent and visionary of these two iconic rock venues. Mr. Graham strategically booked great rock acts each week to fill the seats of both his Fillmore venues ... and fill more seats he did. I attended the Filmore East almost every weekend since the ticket prices were only $3 - $5 to see such acts as Janis Joplin or Jimi Hendrix.

Ten years later, in 1979, I had the pleasure of spending a day with Bill Graham. A tough guy, but a nice guy. He was very open and answered my questions about those "glory days". Proudly, Bill boasted that because of his talent booking expertise at the Fillmore venues, he was hired to help book many of the world-class recording acts to appear at "The Summer of '69s", three iconic outdoor festivals. He shared insight with me explaining his escalating budgeting challenges for indoor venues. He explained that some of the top rock acts were demanding higher and higher performance fees, to a point that Bill barely afford the acts, and still offer low, affordable ticket prices to his Filmore hippy patrons. So now, the next step in rock history was to book acts at large outdoor music festivals since larger attendance crowds could increase overall gross ticket sale income.

UPSTAGE – *Weekends, June 1969* - No cover-charge. Before the large rock music festivals got underway during that amazing summer, and whenever my band wasn't performing on a given weekend, I'd drive *down the shore* to catch some up-and-coming, solo, music artists performing at smaller venues. My favorite was a three-story building called the UPSTAGE in Asbury Park. Downstairs, at "The UPSTAGE", was a small coffee house called, *"The Tea House of the Green Mermaid"*. It offered a tiny, postage-stamp sized, performance space that could only fit one acoustic musician. Upstairs was a larger room where musicians could put their name on a list, and eventually "jam" with other Jersey musicians. That venue supplied a house drum kit, a backline of amplifiers and a house PA system. On many occasions, I'd arrive early, go directly to *The Tea House of the Green Mermaid*, get a seat at a table for one, and park my Fender Jazz bass guitar on the empty seat next to me. To kill time 'til

I could go up and jam upstairs, I'd sit and sip an expresso and listen to a young, fledgling, Bob Dylan-esque singer/guitarist by the name of Bruce Springsteen, (a very talented, very charismatic 19-year-old). He played some covers as well as originals and worked hard to not interrupt the waitresses from gathering their food and tea orders. Sometimes, on his 15-minute break, he'd come over and we'd talk for a minute, and I'd tell him I'd see him upstairs later in the evening to *jam* a bit. The expresso was good and the memories are great. I attended as many times as I could.

ROCK ALL NITE

UPSTAGE CLUB

702 COOKMAN AVE.
ASBURY PARK, N. J.

FRI. & SAT.   PRESENTS   FRI. & SAT.
MAY 21 & 22   MAY 21 & 22

BRUCE SPRINGSTEEN

and the HOT MAMMAS

$1.50   2 SHOWS $1.50
9 – 12 P.M.   1 – 5 A.M.

OPEN EVERY WEEKEND
— NO BOOZE —

TEA HOUSE
OF THE
GREEN MERMAID

OPEN EVERY NITE
YOU MUST BE OVER 17 YRS. OLD TO GET IN

NEWPORT JAZZ FESTIVAL

JULY 3 THRU 6, 1969
AT FESTIVAL FIELD
NEWPORT, R.I.

THURSDAY JULY 3 AT 6 P.M.
FOR THE JAZZ AFICIONADO
GEORGE BENSON QUARTET
KENNY BURRELL QUARTET
BILL EVANS/JEREMY STEIG
YOUNG HOLT UNLIMITED
FREDDIE HUBBARD QUINTET
SUNNY MURRAY QUINTET
ANITA O'DAY
SUN RA SOLAR ARKESTRA
PHIL WOODS AND THE
EUROPEAN RHYTHM MACHINE

FRIDAY JULY 4 AT 2 P.M.
GIANT JAM SESSION: JIMMY SMITH, HOST
including Art Blakey, Benny Green,
Hampton Hawes, Paul Jefferies, Jo Jones,
Albert Mangelsdorff, Howard McGhee,
Ray Nance, Ake Persson, Slam Stewart,
Sonny Stitt, Buddy Tate,
Jimmy Crawford, and others.

FRIDAY JULY 4 AT 8 P.M.
AN EVENING OF JAZZ-ROCK
JEFF BECK
BLOOD, SWEAT AND TEARS
ROLAND KIRK QUARTET
STEVE MARCUS
TEN YEARS AFTER
JETHRO TULL

SATURDAY JULY 5 AT 2 P.M.
GARY BURTON QUARTET
MILES DAVIS QUINTET
JOHN MAYALL
MOTHERS OF INVENTION
NEWPORT ALL STARS with
Red Norvo, Tal Farlow, Ruby Braff,
George Wein, Don Lamond, and
Larry Ridley

SATURDAY JULY 5 AT 8 P.M.
ART BLAKEY QUINTET
DAVE BRUBECK TRIO
WITH GERRY MULLIGAN
STEPHANE GRAPELLI
THE SAVAGE ROSE
SLY AND THE FAMILY STONE
O.C. SMITH
WORLD'S GREATEST JAZZ BAND
With Maxine Sullivan

SUNDAY JULY 6 AT 11 AM
"THE LIGHT IN THE WILDERNESS"
AN ORATORIO BY DAVE BRUBECK
Erich Kunzel, Conductor
Dave Brubeck Trio
Robert Hale, Baritone
David Matthews, Organ
Chorus Pro Musica,
Alfred Nash Patterson, Director

SUNDAY JULY 6 AT 2 P.M.
AN AFTERNOON WITH JAMES BROWN

SUNDAY JULY 6 AT 8 P.M.
SCHLITZ MIXED BAG
WILLIE BOBO SEXTET
HERBIE HANCOCK SEXTET
B.B. KING
BUDDY RICH ORCHESTRA
WINTER
LED ZEPPELIN
The Newport Jazz Festival expresses its appreciation to
Jos. Schlitz Brewing Co. for its generous assistance with
Sunday Evening Concert.

Evening and Sunday Afternoon Tickets
$3.50, $4.50, $5.50, $6.50
Box Seats $10.00
Friday and Saturday Afternoon
Tickets, General Admission $4.00

Do Not Send Cash or Stamps
Mail orders will be filled in order of receipt
Address mail orders to:
Newport Jazz Festival, Newport, R.I. 02840
Tel. (401) 846-5500

FESTIVALS PRODUCED BY FESTIVAL PRODUCTIONS, INC.
MORGAN STATE JAZZ FESTIVAL, June 21, 22, Morgan State College, Baltimore, Md.
HAMPTON JAZZ FESTIVAL, June 26-29, Hampton Institute, Hampton, Va.

NEWPORT JAZZ FESTIVAL

NEWPORT JAZZ FESTIVAL – *July 3, 4, 5, 6, 1969*
Ticket prices were $3.50 per day. As the summer of '69 heated up and we sizzled into July, telephone pole posters freely advertised the upcoming festivals. It was a new era where rock acts were now being included into the roster of the old, established jazz line-ups of The Newport Jazz Festival in Newport, Rhode Island. Newport was only a three-hour drive from midtown Manhattan. Rock-style acts like Jeff Beck, Canned Heat, Iron Butterfly, Procol Harem, Blood, Sweat & Tears, Three Dog Night, Chicago, The Chambers Brothers and even Joe Cocker were now included on that Newport bill.

Huge crowds. The attendance estimates topped 10,000 with another 20,000 that couldn't get in, so they had to listen from an adjoining area. Luckily, I arrived two days earlier, so I was able to set my ripped, blue-jeaned butt down in the field about thirty feet from the stage.

Amazing shows. The last of three evenings hosted the first-ever, east-coast appearance of a newer group from England called Led Zeppelin. The group performed for two hours with Jimmy Page playing guitar with a violin bow, while vocal-acrobat Robert Plant belted and climbed "The Stairway to Heaven." Incredible memory. (To think, only one year earlier found me in Newport R.I. in my military issued U.S. Navy blues, freezing in my winter, pea-coat, stationed throughout the winter months on the USS Coates, a destroy escort ship left over from World War II.)

MOON SHOT – *JULY 20, 1969* - As a point of reference, and to make "the summer of '69" even more memorable, Neil Armstrong was the first man to land on the moon.

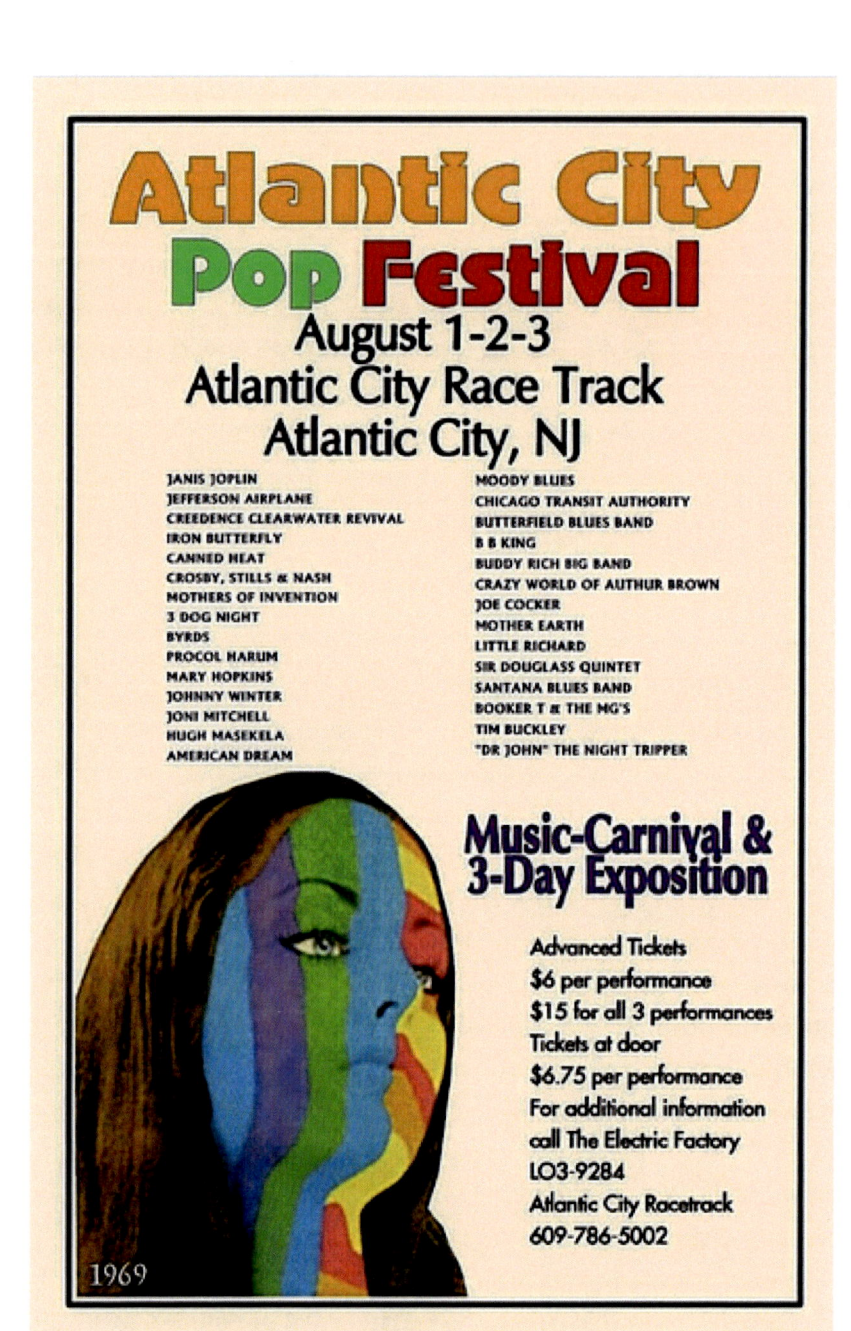

ATLANTIC CITY POP FESTIVAL

ATLANTIC CITY POP FESTIVAL - *Aug 1, 2, 3, 1969* - Ticket prices were $6 each day, or three days for $15. Next in line during the very hot Summer of '69 was the Atlantic City Pop Festival held at the Atlantic City Racecourse in Mays Landing, NJ. This time I arrived three days early. Attendance estimates were approx. 150,000. Acts included Janis Joplin, Jefferson Airplane, Joni Mitchell, Joe Cocker, Little Richard, Booker T and the M. G's, The Byrds, Santana, Frank Zappa and Dr. John. Throughout the evening hours I listened intently, and then we all went to the Atlantic City beachfront and slept on the sand next to the pounding beach waves until the sun came up to start the next day.

WOODSTOCK MUSIC & ART FAIR

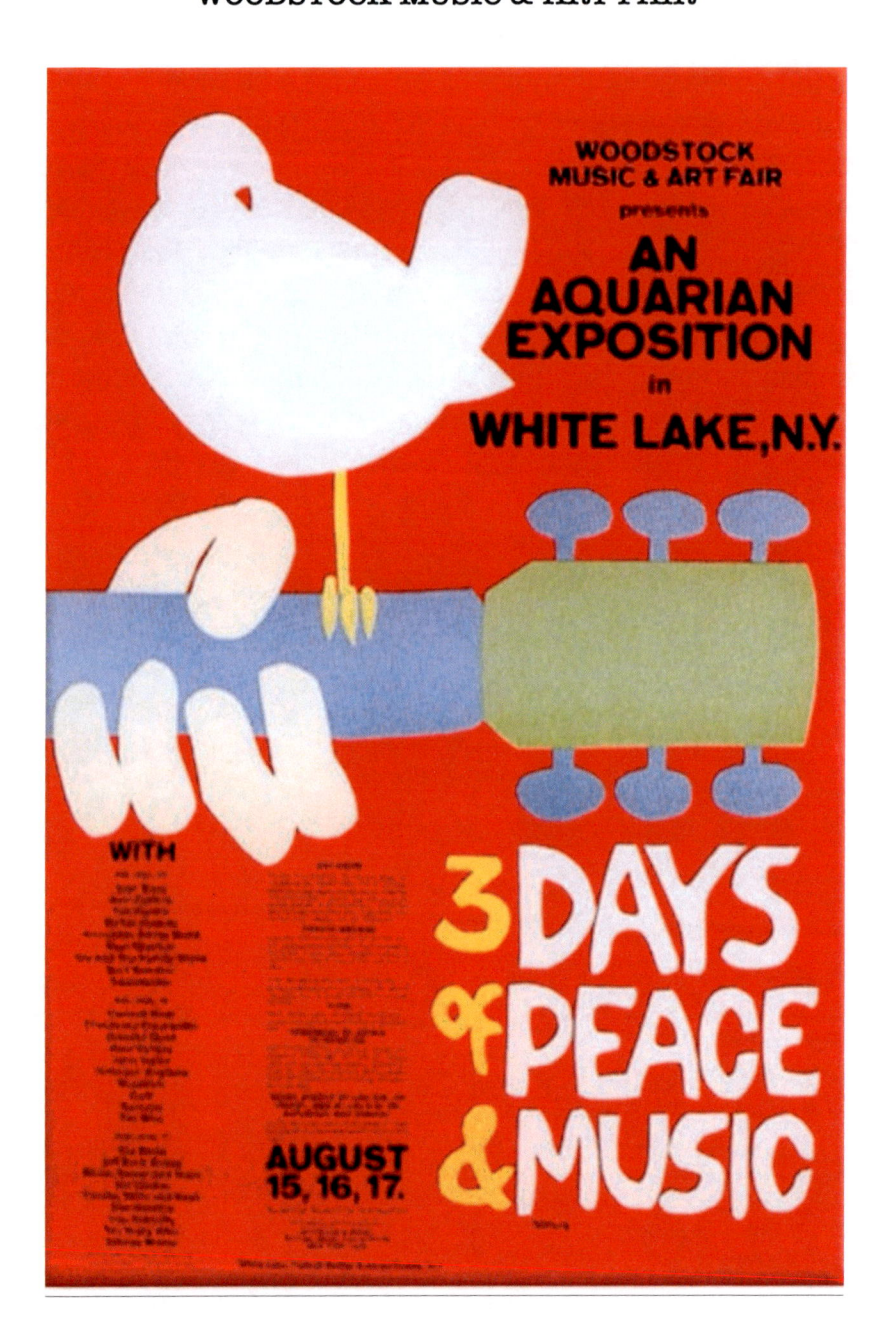

A Gift of Love & Laughter

WOODSTOCK- *August 15,16,17, 1969*

This was the ULTIMATE music festival of the 20th century. For this festival I purchased tickets six weeks prior to the event's start. Along with my friends, Duke, Tom and Pumpkin, the four of us drove up on the New York State Thruway to Woodstock, NY in Duke's small, light brown, four-gear, stick shift, Volkswagen, stuffed with four, old sleeping bags, and a sack of new peanut butter and jelly sandwiches for each of us. This time, we arrived five days early. However, the festival was officially relocated from Woodstock, NY to Max Yasger's dairy farm near Bethel, NY. Unfortunately, we didn't know where Max Yasger's farm was located. However, ... just as we departed the original (now canceled) festival location, we saw an old pickup truck filled with a load of wooden, directional, road arrows. (Each sign had a stenciled dove on a guitar neck painted on it.) We decided to follow that truck, which we were told was heading to the new festival location. At each turn, the old hippy driver would get out from the driver's side, grab a sign, and hammer a sign into the ground. These signs signified the direction to the new festival location. All in all, this took us about three hours to drive from the old festival grounds to the new festival grounds.

Upon arriving at Max Yasgur's dairy farm (the new festival site), there appeared to be about 20,000 young long-haired hippies, puffing away in the grass-filled, dairy farm field (*if you know what I mean*). Even though we arrived five days early, we still had to park the VW approximately a football field away from the front of the performance stage. I found and declared my own tiny little piece of real estate (which became my temporary home for four days), which proved good enough to see the faces of the performers. I plunked myself down and made myself at home. That was the last time I saw my other three buddies, and the last time I saw that VW.

When we arrived at the exact site of the festival, I noticed that there had not been a security/boundary fence erected yet. (Eventually, a small chain link fence was lightly planted around the perimeter of the festival area, but it was only three feet high, and the attendees were much higher/taller than that.) Anyone pushing it forward could easily have knocked it over. As darkness came upon the area, parties continued, the music rocked, and the marijuana was rolled. I decided to grab some ... sleep.

When the sun slowly rose the next morning, my eyes focused on my surroundings, and I realized that an additional 100,000 blue jean-clad, long-haired hippies must have arrived throughout the night. The slopping hill behind me became a mountain of people. I never knew until that moment, how many people loved to listen to live music as much as I did.

Frantically, the performance stage was being built. The area was filled with the sound of excessive, rapid-fire hammering. I was amazed how quickly the stage and the metal, side towers that supported the spotlights and speakers, were being erected. There were constant messages sent over the loudspeaker PA system, some looking to rejoin friends (instructed to meet near the stage), some to caution people not to take the red LSD, and others announcing info about where the Porto-Johns were located, or where you could buy some food. I remember an MC introducing himself as *Wavy Gravy*. To the best of my recollection, I remember an announcement stating that the NY Thruway was now closed, and we are now the third largest populated area in the State of New York. Then came a big announcement: *"The fences have all been torn down and this is now officially a FREE CONCERT."* I kept my tickets in my blue jean pocket and I still have, to this day, my tickets as a souvenir.

Day #1 - The day started off between seventy-nine and eighty-three Fahrenheit. It was dry but early on, low clouds were forming, and showers were expected for the following day. The acts started. The audience focus was directed to the stage. Richie Havens was the first act, and he was wonderful. Act by act the lineup proved fabulous. The first day brought the folk artists, and one by one, the show unfolded. I've often heard it quipped, *"if you remember the sixties, then you weren't really there!"* Well, I was there, and I remember it well: Richie Havens, Sweetwater, Melanie, Ravi Shankar, Arlo Guthrie, Joan Baez.

Day #2 – Once the music started, it ever stopped. Each act just got better and better and more intense: Country Joe and the Fish, John Sebastian, Santana, Canned Heat, Grateful Dead, Leslie West & Mountain, Creedence Clearwater Revival, Janis Joplin, Sly & The Family Stone, The WHO and Jefferson Airplane. I remember it felt like the entire mountain of people was actually moving when Sly and the Family Stone played, "Dance to the Music". John Fogerty, along with Creedence Clearwater Revival rocked that stage like no other act. Janis Joplin was absolutely mesmerizing.

Day #3 - The day began with Joe Cocker taking the stage. Just shortly after Joe finished his performance, a large thunderstorm approached near the venue. I remember seeing the black clouds head right towards us, but then, they just passed us by. I think everyone thought we were going to be saved ... not so. There were wild lightning hits and strong winds that quickly came upon us. Organizers were frantically forced to cover precious electronic equipment, as well as moving people off the stage, and off the huge metal, lighting towers that surrounded it. Max Yasgur's fields were transformed into a sea of mud, and subsequently destroyed by the crowd of half a million people. The storms delayed the performance until approximately 6:30pm. The damp and muddy conditions thinned the crowds, but the music started up again. It just kept continuing throughout the night: Ten Years After, Blood Sweat and Tears, Crosby, Stills Nash & Young and then the final act, the closing act ... Jimi Hendrix.

Since the crowd had thinned out quite a bit, I was able to get about forty feet from the stage when a lone, electric guitar solo started playing which seemed to encourage the sun to peak its head up even higher. It was Jimi Hendrix playing the most incredible electric rock version of The STAR-SPANGLED BANNER. Jimi was the featured closing act. NO ONE could follow him. He played for about thirty-minutes, and then the festival was over. I stopped to look around.

Mud was everywhere, as well as soaking wet sleeping bags, shirts, shoes, blankets, ripped up plastic garbage bags strewn all over Max Yasgur's farm. Some people started to dive and slide down the hill in the mud. It was hard to believe that it was actually over. I noticed that some people started to pick up the mess and put it into piles. I helped. We did that for about four hours, then my energy was totally zapped with no clue as to how I would make it back home. I was completely drenched, but I felt baptized. My clothing was filled with mud. My ears filled with music. My mind filled with memories. My heart filled with love.

I looked around. I found my own walking path to a back road. Out of nowhere, a flower painted VW bus pulled up and asked if I wanted a ride. They drove me 100 miles, all the way back to my NJ home, right to my front door. I remember standing outside my family's side door, where I stopped and pondered. I acknowledged to myself that I was a changed teenager. I would never be the same after that experience ... and I never was. I realized that I wasn't alone in my thinking. I realized I was part of a new generation that had the power to alter the course of history. For one brief weekend, I escaped the national turmoil of presidential assassinations, war, civil rights and the threat of losing my freedom. I learned that during a disaster, people could all work together peacefully. It was there that I decided to follow my dream ... and I did just that ... I pursued my dream to be a clown and help spread love and laughter. Like Jimi Hendrix asked ... Are you experienced? Yes, Jimi, I was.

Peace & Love

Since Woodstock became a *Free Concert*, I was able to keep my tickets, and I still have them.

WOODSTOCK MUSIC and ART FAIR
FRIDAY
AUGUST 15, 1969
10:00 A. M.
$8.00 Good For One Admission Only
03115 A NO REFUNDS GLOBE TICKET COMPANY

FRI.
AUG. 15
1969
03115 A

WOODSTOCK MUSIC and ART FAIR
SATURDAY
AUGUST 16, 1969
10:00 A. M.
$7.00 Good For One Admission Only
A 01209 NO REFUNDS GLOBE TICKET COMPANY

WOODSTOCK MUSIC and ART FAIR
SUNDAY
AUGUST 17, 1969
10:00 A. M.
$7.00 Good For One Admission Only
A 01165 NO REFUNDS GLOBE TICKET COMPANY

A Gift of Love & Laughter

After that experience, I searched through magazine articles, newspaper stories, books, press photos, album covers, etc. but could never find a photo of myself at Woodstock ... until just recently. Here's a picture of me in the crowd while Jimi Hendrix played the Star-Spangled Banner.

(Photo on right – I'm in the center with the long hair.)

It had been rumored that other top act like the Rolling Stones, The Doors, John Lennon, and Bob Dylan all individually declined to perform at Woodstock, because many of those acts had demanded to be paid in full, in cash, before they each went on stage.

In order to get Jimi Hendrix to perform, the festival organizers had to convince a local banker to open up after hours and arrange for an emergency loan. It is also reported that a clause was ultimately included within Jimi Hendrix's contract stipulating that no act could be scheduled to perform after Jimi. As history has reported, no one did perform after Jimi. He performed on the fourth day of a three-day festival...and the rest is in the history books in various degrees of similarity.

Here's the reported list of act compensations:

Jimi Hendrix = $18,000
Blood Sweat and Tears = $15,000
Creedence Clearwater Revival = $10,000
Joan Baez = $10,000
Jefferson Airplane = $7,500
The Band = $7,500
Janis Joplin = $7,500
Richie Havens = $7,000
Sly and the Family Stone = $7,000
Canned Heat = $6,000
The WHO = $6,000
Arlo Guthrie = $5,000
Crosby, Stills, Nash & Young = $5,000
Ravi Shankar = $4,500
Johnny Winter = $3,750
Ten Years After = $3,250
Country Joe and the Fish = $2,500
The Grateful Dead = $2,500
Mountain = $2,000
Tim Hardin = $2,000
Joe Cocker = $1,375
Sweetwater = $1,250
John Sebastian = $1,000
Melanie = $750
Santana = $750
Sha Na Na = $700
Quill = $375

Ron Severini
11/3/2020
Union, N.J.

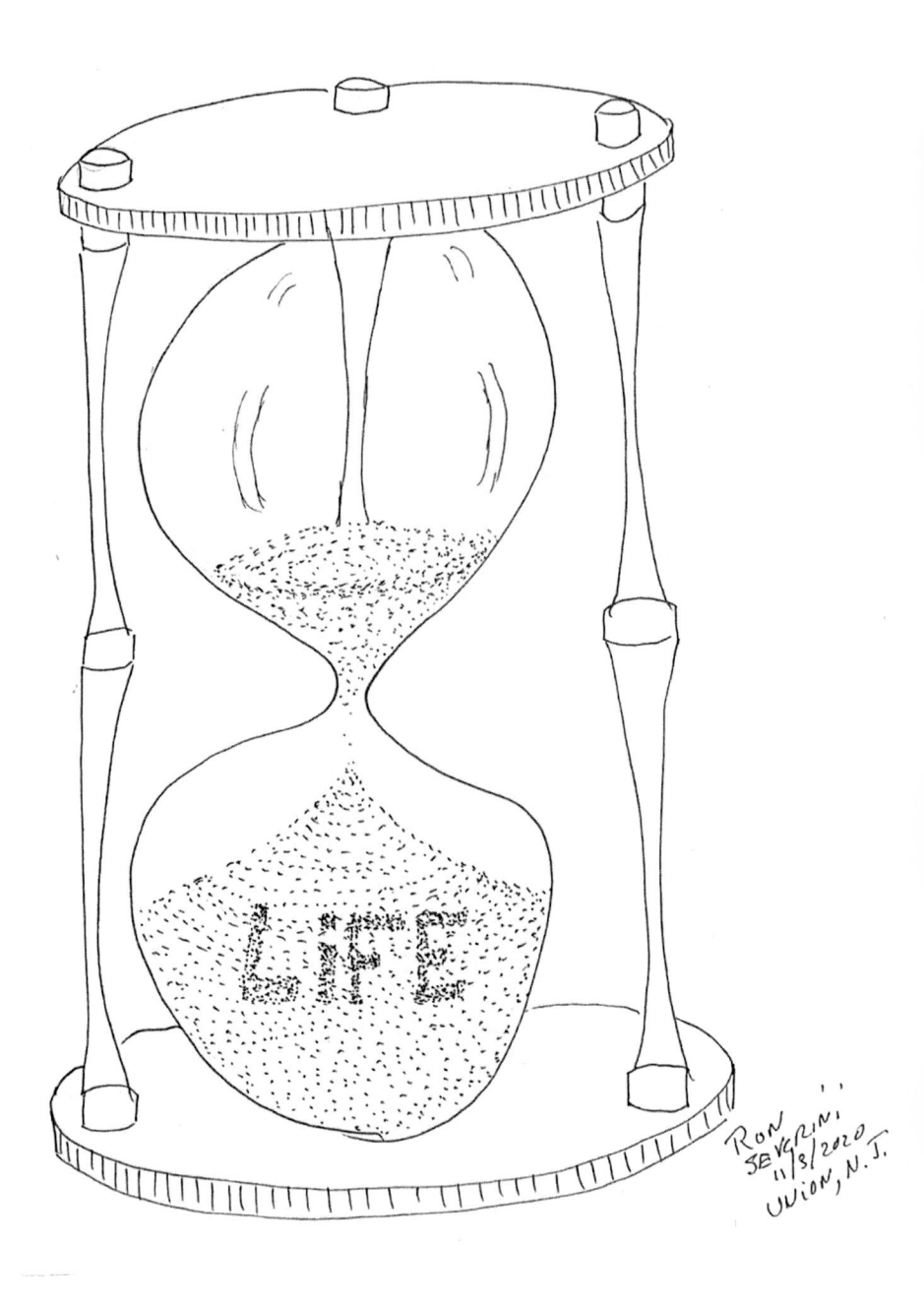

IT'S ABOUT TIME

Tick Tick Tick Tick Tick Tick Tick Tick Tick Tick Tick Tick Tick Tick Tick Tick Tick Tick Tick Tick Tick Tick Tick Tick Tick Tick Tick Tick Tick Tick Tick Tick Tick Tick Tick Tick Tick Tick Tick Tick Tick Tick Tick Tick Tick Tick Tick Tick Tick Tick Tick Tick Tick Tick Tick Tick Tick ...

There are sixty, clicking, ticking, clock clicks in each minute ... Always have been ... Always will be ... I shall invest two of those minutes to share a story ... A story about *time* ... So, start the clock ...

Once upon a *time* ... I was much younger.

During those formative years, I vividly remember my little, old Italian grandmother sitting me down at the dinner table after a tasty, homemade pasta meal and offering me her sage advice. Then, she capped it off with her decadent, homemade cannoli. She'd speak in her cute, little broken English and say things like: *"Always remember that time, she's-ah precious"* and *"Life, she's-ah short"* and *"Some-ah day you're ah-gonna realize that time-ah just goes by too darn-ah fast!"*

She also offered profound words of wisdom like: *"Lost time, she's-ah never gonna be found-ah no more"* and even, *"Time, she waits for-ah no-bodddy!"* She always suggested to me: *"My little darlin'* ... *never, ever, getta old."* I didn't really know what to do with that piece of advice (and confidentially, I didn't really want to sit there and think about it back then) but in *time*, I eventually came to the realization that she was a very wise, astute, little Italian immigrant ... (Well, most of the *time*. Someday I'll tell you the story about the *time* she thought she bought a brand-new color TV for ten dollars).

Anyway, having been born between the years 1946 and 1964 makes me a baby boomer. Back in those "Sensational 60's" I was told that I was a boarder-line radical, and anyone over the age of thirty was not to be trusted. However, as time marched on, I evolved and matured ... Slowly, I too reached, and passed that 30-year-old mile marker. Somewhere along life's highway, I turned into my parents, and now, I've slowly turned into my grandparents, one chin at a time ... *Time* really does keep ticking. My grandfather, may he rest in peace, used to quip: *"Life she's-ah like da roll of da toilet paper ... The closer you getta to da end, the faster she goes!"*

Reminiscing about those earlier *times*, whether I was *marking time, making time, doing time* or *killing time*, I proceeded with the comforting knowledge that Mick Jagger assuredly sang *"Time is on my side."* Conversely, Bob Dylan sang in *three-quarter time, "The Times they are a changing."* Ironically, both artists and their music have withstood *the test of time.*

My life's goal has always been to be as healthy and as happy as I can be, for as many days as possible. Eating healthy, walking daily and trying to stay positive is how I invest some of my awake *time*. I try to smile every day. I try to make somebody laugh every day. I'm happy. So far, so good. I'm enjoying my *family time, fun time, creative time* and *travel time.*

Looking back at it all, I did learn that *"time is money"* and *"time is of the essence."* Whether I was paid *straight time, time and a half* or *double time,* whether I punched a *time clock*, logged that *drive time*, filled in that *time sheet* or needed to explain my *time* to the *timekeeper*, (who was keeping those *time cards*) or even now, whether it's *daytime, nighttime, work time, lunchtime, on time, off time, nap time, vacation time,* be it in the *springtime, summertime, autumn-time* or *wintertime,* no matter what *time zone* I am located, it's always *high time* to make the most of *my time*, to stop *wasting time* and *"let the good times roll!"*

My *time* is not up, and my *time* is not over, and neither is yours. Like my grandmother's thought-provoking advice stated: "*Time, she's ah da most precious ah-gift.*" So, with life having an unknown expiration date, and since *time* is short, the *time* has come for me, and for you to do something about *time* ... and *it's about time* we did!

So, it's "*Showtime!*" "*There's no time like the present.*" "*Times a ticking!*" Yesterday's gone, and tomorrow hasn't arrived yet. It's my *time*, and it can be your *time!* It's about today, and as my grandmother also used to say, "*Time, she's ah the most valuable thing somebody she can-ah spend!*"

So, I hope the *time* you've spent in reading my little story has been *time* you feel was well spent. If so, then maybe *it's about time* that you invest some additional *time* in talking with a grandparent. Grandparents can be very smart people!

Well, where has the *time* gone? Looks like I'm now out of *time*. So, till next *time* ... I hope you take one day at a *time* and live a very happy, healthy, long *time*!

Tick Tick Tick Tick Tick Tick Tick Tick Tick Tick Tick Tick Tick Tick Tick Tick Tick Tick Tick Tick Tick Tick Tick Tick Tick Tick Tick Tick Tick Tick Tick Tick Tick Tick Tick Tick ...

Tick Tick Tick Tick Tick Tick Tick Tick Tick Tick Tick Tick Tick Tick Tick Tick Tick Tick Tick Tick Tick Tick ...

Time to write this story: 4-hours
Time to re-write this story: 12-hours
Time to read this story: 2-minutes

My little Italian "Philosopher" Grandmother
known to all her friends, simply as:
JOSIE

A Gift of Love & Laughter

Time to eat one of:
JOSIE'S FAMOUS
CANNOLIS

JOSIE made the BEST tasting CANNOLIS on the Planet!

TIME

100 YEARS:
100 Years = 36,500 Days
100 Years = 876,000 Hours
100 Years = 52,560,000 Minutes
100 Years = 3,153,600,000 Seconds

10 YEARS:
10 Years = 3,650 Days
10 Years = 87,600 Hours
10 Years = 5,256,000 Minutes
10 Years = 315,360,000 Seconds

1 YEAR:
1 Year = 365 Days
1 Year = 8,760 Hours
1 Year = 525,600 Minutes
1 Year = 31,536,000 Seconds

1 DAY:
1 Day = 24 Hours
1 Day = 1,440 Minutes
1 Day = 86,400 Minutes
1 Day = 5,184,000 Seconds

1 HOUR:
1 Hour = 60 Minutes
1 Hour = 3,600 Seconds

1 MINUTE:
1 Minute = 60 Seconds

LIFE IS SHORT

Life is Short ... Eat the cannoli

Life is Short ... Buy the shoes

Life is Short ... Take the day off

Life is Short ... Take a bubble bath

Life is Short ... Take a ride through the mountains

Life is Short ... Get a massage

Life is Short ... Go read a book

Life is Short ... Take a deep breath in a flower shop

Life is Short ... Go shopping

Life is Short ... Go to the beach

Life is Short ... Go to a museum

Life is Short ... Go to the circus

Life is Short ... Plan a dream vacation

Life is Short ... Quit your day job and do what you really want to do in your life.

TWENTIETH CENTURY SLANG

There were five distinct and unique generations of Americans throughout the one hundred years that encompassed the Twentieth Century. Within each of those generational categories, a subculture of teenagers existed, each finding a need to develop their own verbal jargon of slang words and phrases.

Here's a basic timetable break-down of the five generational categories. Please note each lasted approximately fourteen to twenty-four years:

1900 – 1924 ... "The Greatest Generation"
1925 – 1945 ... "The Silent Generation"
1946 – 1964 ... "The Baby Boomers"
1965 – 1979 ... "Generation X"
1980 – 2000 ... "Millennials" or "Generation Y"

Young adults of the day always seemed to create their own brand of clever communication. For example, the evolution of twentieth century American slang went from *"The Bee's Knees"* and *"Twenty-Three Skidoo"* during the earlier part of the century ... to *"Hip," "Cool"* and *"Groovy"* in the mid-part of the century ... to *"Bad," "Solid"* and *"Awesome"* at the end of the century.

Slang words and phrases are almost impossible to track down and identify because their exact origin of who, where or when they were created is unknown. What we do know is

A Gift of Love & Laughter

most of them found their way from young, ethnic, and social minority subcultures to later become popularized in the mainstream culture of everyday American conversation.

For your amusement and enjoyment, I have researched, gathered, and listed many slang words and phrases within this musing. In doing so, I discovered that each generation found a need to create their own brand of slang within the same basic broad categories: Money, Sex, Likes, Dis-likes, Looks, Intelligence, Good, Bad, Home, Speed, Transportation, Communication, Coming, Going, Clothes, etc.

One of the most *"Slang-ified"* words in the English language is the word MONEY. Someone referring to a one-dollar bill can call it a *"Single,"* a *"Buck,"* an *"Ace,"* a *"Bean"* or a *"Bone."* A two-dollar bill has been referred to as a *"Deuce"* or a *"Tom."* A five-dollar bill was often called a *"Fin,"* *"Five-spot,"* *"Fiver"* or a *"Nickel."* A ten-dollar bill has been called a *"Sawbuck,"* *"Ten-spot,"* *"Hamilton"* or a *"Dime."* A twenty-dollar bill has been replaced by a *"Jackson"* or a *"Double Sawbuck,"* and a one-hundred-dollar bill, a *"C-Note,"* a *"Benjamin,"* a *"Benny"* or a *"Yard."*

Whether it's included in a conversation on a telephone, on a street corner, in a bar or back alley, on a phone call with a loan shark, with a stock broker, in a book, movie or even on a TV episode of the Soprano's, you may have heard the word MONEY referred to as *"Bread," "Bucks," "Bacon," "Bankroll," "Cash," "Coin," "Change," "Cabbage," "Clams," "Cake," "Chips," "Chump-Change," "Dough," "Funds," "Grease," "Green," "Loot," "Moolah," "Paper," "Quid," "Salad," "Stash," "Scratch," "Smackers"* or even *"Simoleons!"*

Next, there's been a plethora of slang words, terms or phrases that signify someone either likes something or somebody; or they give their approval of something; or it simply means "I LIKE IT." For instance ... that's *"Hip,"* that's *"Hep,"* that's *"Jake,"* it's all *"Copacetic,"* it's the *"Bee's Knee's,"* the *"Cat's Pajama's,"* or it's a *"Gas,"* I can *"Dig It,"* like *"Wow," "Far Out," "Way Out," "Mind-Blowing," "Outta Sight," "Dynamite," "Decent," "Neat," "Smooth," "Sweet," "Solid," "Bad," "Rad," "Wicked," "Groovy,"* a *"Blast,"* the *"Bomb," "Hot," "Cool," "Crazy," "Classic," "Choice,"* and in more recent days they are using the word *"Awesome!"*

And if someone wanted to say, "I DON'T LIKE IT," they could also say ... that's *"Gross," "Grody,"* or *"Germsville,"* or that's *"Yucko," "Putrid"* or *"Gnarly."* Other examples are *"a Real Drag,"* it's *"Squareville," "L-7,"* or *"Gag me with a Spoon,";* or if someone else doesn't like something, you might tell them; *"Don't Flip Your Wig,"* don't have a *"Conniption Fit,"* don't *"Go Postal,"* or don't *"Have a Cow!"*

Now, while researching all of this, I found it immensely amusing; thus, I've created a little poem incorporating some of the many memorable slang words and phrases popularized during that century-long period. I hope you enjoy it, or should I say I hope you *"dig it,"* or find it *"bad," "rad," "hip," "hot," "cool," "heavy," "far out," "out of sight,"* or *"dynamite!"*

A TWENTIETH CENTURY SLANG POEM

"COOL"... "WITH IT"... "JUMPIN' JIVE,"
"KNUCKLE SANDWICH"... "HIP"... "HIGH FIVE"

"BLAST FROM THE PAST"... "OUTTA SIGHT,"
"It's REAL GONE"... "It's DYNAMITE"

"BURNIN' RUBBER"... "CRUSIN FOR A BRUISIN,"
"PART TIME LOVER"... "CAN'T WIN FOR LOSING"

"A BUMMER"... "A BADDIE"... "The CAT'S PAJAMA,"
"WHO'S YOUR DADDY?"... "I AIN'T YOUR MOMMA"

"PARTY HARDY"... "HAMMERED or SMASHED,"
"TANKED"... "KNOCKERED"... "TWISTED or TRASHED"

"VEG OUT"... "BOUNCE"... "LET IT RIDE,"
"BLOW THIS JOINT"... "CATCH YOU ON THE FLIP-SIDE"

"RAD"... "SMOOTH"... "A REAL BAD BOY,"
"The MAN"... "The BOSS"... "The REAL MCCOY"

"FAB"... "DOPE"... "CHOICE"... "The BOMB,"
"NOWHERE"... "SPLITSVILLE"... "KEEP ON KEEPIN' ON"

"LAY IT ON ME"... "SLIP ME SOME SKIN,"
"CHECK IT"... and "LOOK WHAT THE CAT DRAGGED IN"

"GONE"... "WACKED"... "In the TWILIGHT ZONE,"

"The LIGHTS ARE OUT and NOBODY'S HOME"
"It's IN THE BAG" ... "It's SOLID" ... "It's PHAT,"
"Got it MADE IN THE SHADE" ... "He's a REAL COOL CAT"

"CHROME DOME" ... "LONG HAIR" ... "FREAKIN' TRIPPY,"
"LOVE CHILD" ... "DUDE" ... "PSYCHEDELIC HIPPIE"

"BUST A GUT" ... "BUST A MOVE,"
It's all "COPECETIC" ... "Get IN THE GROOVE"

"WICKED" ... "AWESOME" ... "SUPER DOOPER,"
"GNARLY" ... "PREPPY" ... "A PARTY POOPER"

She's "A REAL HUMDINGER" ... "HE AINT NO GIFT,"
"A DIME STORE MELTDOWN" ... "CATCH MY DRIFT"

"DO ME A SOLID" ... "CUT ME SOME SLACK,"
"LAY IT ON ME" ... Or "JUMP BACK JACK"

"SPLIT THIS SCENE" ... "GO-MAN-GO,"
Let's "BLOW THIS JOINT" ... "DADDY-O"

It's all so "GROOVY" ... "I CAN DIG IT,"
So, "BET THE FARM" ... and "GET JIGGY WITH IT!!!"

YADA YADA YADA

YOU CAN'T GO BACK

You can't go back and start over.

It is impossible to change the beginning.

It is impossible to change the middle.

However, you can start from where you are right now,

... and change the ending.

When it comes time to write your life story,
nobody should be sitting at the typewriter but YOU.

SPRING LAKE, NEW JERSEY

A place to dream

DOWN THE SHORE

Soft, Still, Serene, and Soothing,

Peaceful, Placid, Pure and Pleasing,

Tranquil, Tempered, Tender and Touching,

Undisturbed, Unruffled, Understood and Unassuming,

Cool, Calm, Comforted and Composed,

Dainty, Delicate, Dim and Demure,

Gentle, Mild, Moderate and Meditative,

Friendly, Charming, Quiet, and Reflective.

*"I shall always find comfort
in the rhythm of the sea."*

DREAMS

I woke up this morning
from a magical dream,
but it vanished right out of my head,
and as hard as I tried
to return back to sleep
I only kept yawning instead.

I tightened my eyes shut,
I took a deep breath,
and I tried to re-enter that dream,
but the harder I tried
to sink back in deep sleep
my attempt was so futile it seemed.

I lay there awake now
with thought to myself
where did that dream really go?
This was a puzzle I started to ponder,
something I now had to know.

I looked under my pillow,
looked under my sheet,
I even looked under my bed,
then suddenly realized
A wonderful thought
that my dream never did leave my head.

Stored in my mind now
quietly resting,
secretly hiding alone,
making me happy,
making me think more,
and making me now write this poem.

Is this dream premonition
or hidden desire
or subconsciously some kind of clue?
Self-wishing for insight
or clue for tomorrow
and will it soon ever come true?
Did it choose to come visit
in the wee morning hour
from going to bed very late?
Or due to emotion, or yearning or craving,
or simply from something I ate?

I believe while I'm sleeping
one night in the future
this dream will revisit again,
it's then I will welcome its return, oh so dearly,
as I would an old childhood friend.

Till then it rests safely
stored inside my mind bank,
secured on my private dream shelf,
for I've finally learned
that my dreams are my own
special secrets I keep from myself!

SLEEP

Even as a child I disliked sleeping. I felt I had so much ahead of me to accomplish in my life and sleeping only felt like a waste of my time. Just thinking about sleeping eight hours of every night (one third of my life) seemed so very unproductive. Then one day, my mother sat me down and told me that sleeping was very healthy. She said that since the human body must sleep to recharge itself, I may as well enjoy it and invest in dreaming because dreaming can sometimes lead to fabulous adventures. She said, *"Dreaming was like being in my own fantasy movie, and I was the lead character."* She suggested that I welcome each new sleep night with open arms (except the two I wrap around my pillow) and dream happy, magical thoughts. I did it. I even dreamt I could fly one night. Then she said, *"When you dream a dream that is so wonderful that you may actually want to pursue during your waking hours, just go for it ... and make those dreams come true."* So, I did just that. Life's been a pursuit of trying to make one dream after the next come true. So far, so good. Putting this book together was a dream that I had had one night and now, this book is literally a dream come true. *So, don't give up on your dreams.* Keep sleeping!

Since sleeping (as well as napping) is one thing that we all have in common, I thought I'd do a little research on what some people have to say about it. Thus, I've gathered and included some various thoughts about sleeping.

I hope you enjoy reading these quotes....

"The amount of sleep required by the average person is five minutes more."
WILSON MIZENER

"Laugh and the world laughs with you, snore and you sleep alone."
ANTHONY BURGESS

"When every inch of the world is known, sleep may be the only wilderness that we have left."
LOUISE ERDRICH

"I think sleeping was my problem in school. If school had started at four in the afternoon, I'd be a college graduate today."
GEORGE FOREMEN

"I heard you snoring in your sleep last night. You must have been dreaming you were taking trombone lessons."
RON SEVERINI

"You're a dirty, little stay in bed, pulling the covers over your head, not listening to what your momma said, 'cause you're a dirty, little stay in bed."
RON SEVERINI

FOLLOW YOUR DREAMS

*"A dream is a wish your heart makes
when you're fast asleep
In dreams you will lose your heartaches
whatever you wish for, you keep"*
CINDERELLA

A WISH ... is just a dream if you do not attach a goal.

A GOAL ... is a dream that can come true if you set a deadline.

A DEADLINE ... is a realistic time limit you set for your goal to be completed.

PLAN OF ACTION ... is your blueprint listing each step-by-step action item to follow.

PASSION & PURPOSE ... is your uncontrollable heart-felt emotion and reason why you want to fulfill your dream.

SUCCESS ... completing your plan and making your own dream come true.

A Gift of Love & Laughter

MY DREAM

TODAY is a HAPPY DAY - TODAY is a SPECIAL Day
TODAY is MY Day

TODAY, I am going to start to make
MY DREAM come true for myself.

MY DREAM is to:

_____
_____

DREAM IT ... BELIEVE IT ... VISUALIZE IT
PLAN IT ... WORK IT ... COMPLETE IT
ENJOY IT ... BE PROUD OF IT
DO IT!!!

First, I'll put together a smart, step-by-step plan.

Next, I'll set a realistic deadline.

MY DREAM shall come true no later than:
_____/_____/_____

Making MY DREAM come true means:

_____

When I do make MY DREAM come true,
I will feel:

_____

The MIGHTY Oak

The MIGHTY OAK

"Great Oaks from little acorns grew,

So, when you're feeling blue,

Remember that the Mighty Oak

Was once a nut like you!"

ALSO

"Remember, ...
The MIGHTY Oak grows stronger
after a natural disaster,
and diamonds are made under pressure."

AND ALSO REMEMBER ...

"NOAH had no boat building experience
Before he built the ARK.
An experienced team of professional ship builders
built the TITANIC."

PLAN "A"

If *"PLAN A"* does not work,
there are still twenty-five more letters
in the alphabet.

A Gift of Love & Laughter

PLAN "BE"

Be Healthy, Be Happy, Be Kind and Be Brave;
Be Calm, Be Patient, Be Smart and Behave.

Be Friendly, Be Helpful, Be Trustworthy, Be Good;
Be Organized, Be Prepared like a safe boy scout should.

Be Courageous, Be Outrageous, Be Adventurous,
Be Daring;

Be Tireless, Be Serious, Be Harmonious, Be Caring.

Be Passionate, Be Obedient, Be Observant, Be Strong;
Be Astute to know when you're right or you're wrong.

Be Big, don't Belittle, Be all you can Be;
Be Content to Be you and Respect that I'm me.

Be Honorable, Be Punctual, Be Clean, Be Immaculate;
Be Believable, Be Approachable, Be Habitually Accurate.

Be Thrifty but Giving, Be Honest of what you see;
And always Be Reminded that the Truth sets you Free.

Be Loyal, Be Hard-Working, Be Serious, yet Be Funny;
Be Driven by your Passion, don't live life just for money.

Be Cheerful, Be Purposeful, Be Remorseful, Be Driven;
Be Thankful for Strengths and real-eyes
they're God-Given.

Be guided by Shakespeare's *"To Be or Not to Be"*;
Be the one and only sculptor that carves your Destiny.

So, Be Bold and Be Original and Be Ecstatic to Be You;
And above all Be Reminded *"To thine own self, BE True!"*

IT'S NEVER TOO LATE

On the day I turned eighteen, I had a self-defeated flash/thought that I was already over the hill, and it was now too late for me to become a child prodigy. What would I do now? I always had an inner passion to be the best musical-comedy performer I could be. I was driven to make my mark in Showbiz. I always loved live, family entertainment, and the variety arts, especially the musical and comedic side of the industry. My real dream was to be a baggy pants burlesque comic, like my hero, Lou Costello, but since vaudeville and burlesque were all but dead in the U.S. during that mid-twentieth century time period, I kept looking to find an alternate opportunity.

I knew I couldn't go back in time, and I knew I couldn't redo anything that happened to me within the first seventeen years of my life, so I decided I'd start the day commemorating the eighteenth year of my birth by enrolling in Manhattan School of Music. The school was in the Harlem area of NYC, right across the river from where I lived in New Jersey. Up until that time, I'd been taking private guitar lessons at a local music school in my hometown. I started those lessons when I was thirteen. I paid for my own lessons by delivering the local town newspaper at 5:00am in the morning. I wanted to learn serious music theory, as well as taking legitimate piano lessons so I could follow my dream.

Our family living room had an old piano that I'd knock around on a bit. I played by ear, and sometimes I would follow a beginner's *"How to teach yourself Piano"* book that I had bought for a dollar.

I learned that I was accepted into Manhattan School of Music and started the program. Each class day I'd arrive early and sit up front. I was always the second student to arrive. There was this little old lady that arrived before me. She'd sit at the classroom piano, practicing and playing the most beautiful piano pieces I had ever heard. Her nimble, little fingers would glide across the keyboard like an Olympic ice skater. After she'd finish playing, the other students would all vigorously applaud her, then the teacher would enter, and the class would begin.

This went on for a month or so. Finally, I decided I would stay after class and introduce myself. Her name was Sarah. I told her how wonderfully she played.

She said, *"THANK YOU, not bad for a seventy-eight-year-old lady, huh?"*

I said, *"seventy-eight, Wow! I just turned eighteen recently and I hope someday to be able to play half as good as you. You probably had been playing piano since you were a kid!"*

She said, *"Actually, NO. On the day I turned seventy-five, I decided to take up piano lessons, and I have been practicing each day ever since."*

SMILE

MAKE 'EM LAUGH

I was a professional circus clown with Ringling Bros and Barnum & Bailey for twenty years. It was my life's ambition and career choice to make people laugh. I wanted to make as many people laugh as possible. I knew I was good at it. I was eager to learn how to make each one of those thousands of people attending every circus show roar in laughter.

When I arrived on the circus lot that very first day, I immediately asked the oldest clown in Clown Alley, *"How could I be as funny as possible?"* I told him that I was determined to create my own signature, one-of-a-kind, clown routines. I asked him, how I would know if what I was brainstorming was going to be funny when developing my own performance material?

His answer ... *"The audience will always tell you if what you've created is funny or not."* With his wisdom of a lifetime of experiences, he simply shared, *"It's really very easy ... if the audience laughs, it's funny, if they don't laugh, it ain't funny!"*

And then he added: *"Although a clown is a fantasy character, you always must be real. You must believe in everything you do; believe in every movement you make. You see, if you don't believe it then the audience ain't gonna believe it, and you wouldn't get the laughter you're after. Being able to make people laugh is a God-given talent. Ya gotta do everything from the bottom of your heart. You gotta give and keep on givin'. You've gotta share your God-given talent. That's why he gave it to you ... to share it. And remember, you ain't there to make their face smile, you're there to make their heart smile."*

Then he wisely offered, *"Keep this in mind kid, you might not always get the audience to respond with a great big belly laugh, and that's ok, 'cause it's also fine if you can get 'em to*

Grin, Giggle, Snicker or Whoop ... Chuckle, Snort, Titter or Chortle ... Crow, Ha Ha, Howl or Shriek ... Scream, Guffaw, Break-up, or Crack-up ... Smile, Burst, Tear in Joy ... or Convulse in Laughter ... And it's also a great sign of laughter success if you can get them to split-a-seam, bust-a-gut and especially, get them 'rolling-in-the-aisles!'"

Then he got up from his dressing trunk, patted me on the back, gave me a wink and said: *"I'm here for ya kid, just let me know if I can help ya! The world needs as many great laugh makers as it can get!"*

LAUGHTER

Laughter just may be the best medicine after all, and it is certainly the least expensive option.

Are you stressed? Are you feeling down? Have you even found yourself a little overweight? Well, it just might be the time to laugh about it.

Laughter is genuinely good for you. To begin, it's said that laughing relieves stress by lowering the levels of the stress hormone cortisol. This can also help relieve physical tension which can help you feel more relaxed. This boosts your immunity, and ultimately, can improve your resistance to disease. Additionally, laughter increases good hormones like endorphins which can reduce temporary pain. Emotional pain can also be alleviated through laughter. Humor can keep you positive. Laughing can improve your mood. It can enhance your resiliency. It's difficult to feel sad when you're laughing.

Laughing can also be good for your heart. Laughter has been proven to have a positive effect on blood pressure, increasing blood flow by expanding the inner lining of the walls of the arteries. Laughing can act as an instant recharger to boost your energy level. Laughing is a lot like exercise. One hearty laugh can burn three to four calories.

A laugh a day may not keep the doctor away, but it can increase your overall well-being. So, giggle, chuckle or snicker! Whatever you do, be sure to LAUGH ABOUT IT!

CIRCLE THE WORDS

Laughter

T	E	A	E	L	H	W	E	L	G	G	I	G	S
E	L	G	H	U	J	H	N	E	H	R	J	E	I
E	I	T	H	A	P	O	I	T	A	H	Z	O	O
L	M	T	S	G	H	O	R	E	I	A	K	R	G
T	S	Y	E	N	U	P	G	B	M	C	I	W	O
R	K	N	E	T	O	A	U	A	U	E	K	O	R
O	S	N	J	N	B	R	L	T	N	R	E	L	T
H	N	U	R	J	T	R	T	M	U	L	S	T	E
C	I	F	N	O	N	E	U	P	K	R	E	T	S
N	C	G	I	Y	K	C	R	C	R	C	C	C	E
R	K	I	A	E	I	R	U	T	N	L	R	K	S
E	E	S	F	S	S	H	M	C	A	E	R	I	U
H	R	N	I	R	C	N	I	S	A	I	C	O	M
U	U	L	H	N	M	H	J	M	A	R	N	C	A

CHUCKLE
AMAZE
GRIN
CHORTLE
ENTERTAIN
SMILE
TICKLE
WHOOP
FUNNY
BURST
SNICKER
HA HA
AMUSE
GIGGLE
LAUGH
SCREAM
JOY
SNORT

A Gift of Love & Laughter

My wish for you ...
"THE LAUGHTER OF A THOUSAND CLOWNS"

HAVE A NICE DAY

Joseph Theodore Smolovecky, aka "Joe the Smo," better known simply as "Joe Smo" was a happy-go-lucky, unemployed, optimistic loser. For example, Joe had been playing the same six lottery numbers each Friday night for the past twenty-six years, never resulting in a winning set of numbers. (He did correctly guess three numbers once and received $5.00 back in return, which he quickly cashed in to purchase another losing ticket.)

Maybe today will be the day that Joe will change his luck.

On this one particular "First Monday of the Month" morning, Joe set his alarm to wake up at 7:00am to get ready to face the world. Unfortunately, Joe slept through that alarm. However, just in case alarm #1 didn't work, Joe also set his backup alarm #2 to blast himself out of bed at 7:30am, and it worked! That day, Joe was awakened at 7:30am to Jon Bon Jovi's hit song, "Have a Nice Day!"

That caused Joe to jump out of bed, slide into his bathroom, quickly wash his face and brush his teeth, and while staring at his medicine cabinet mirror, read the big reminder post-it note he wrote to himself the night before:

BIG JOB INTERVIEW
TODAY at 9:00am
GOOD LUCK JOE!

Hurriedly, Joe pulled on a pair of dirty old pants and a rumpled-up shirt laying on the floor, grabbed his wallet and dry cleaner claim check (also stuck to his medicine cabinet mirror), and flew down his fifth-floor apartment stairs. Making his way to the sidewalk, Joe dashed into the cold and headed directly to his corner dry cleaner to grab his freshly pressed, interview suit he'd been planning to wear for this big occasion.

Joe went into this hole-in-the-wall establishment and handed the man behind the counter his claim check. The dry cleaner handed Joe his suit and after Joe paid the tab, the man cordially said, *"Nice to see you again Joe ... Have a nice day"*.

Before departing the dry-cleaning store, Joe looked at the suit and saw a big burn stain across the entire front of his interview jacket. Disappointed, but keeping his cool, Joe showed the dry cleaner the burn but quickly understood there was nothing the dry cleaner could do now, and it was starting to become late for Joe to make it to his interview.

Again, as Joe was exiting, the dry cleaner politely said, *"Have a nice day!"*

Joe quickly ran back home, flew up the old wooden stairs of his fifth-floor walkup (no elevator), made a beeline to his clothes closet, opened it, and what did he see: the only clothing item still left hanging in his closet was an old, faded, moth-eaten, woolen sweater his blind aunt Sadie had hand-knitted for him twelve years ago for Christmas. With no other available option, Joe put on his newly, dry-cleaned pants, a dress shirt and tie, and to keep warm, good 'ole Aunt Sadie's moth-eaten, good-luck, woolen sweater.

Joe grabbed his resume envelope and flew down those same five flights of turn-of-the-century, wooden stairs and jumped out his apartment house entrance door into the cruel, cold world. He immediately heard thunder as it started to pour rain.

Luckily, Joe saw a street vendor selling umbrellas for $13.00 each but noticed there was only one umbrella left for sale on top of that vendor's make-shift, cardboard table. As Joe grabbed for that last remaining umbrella, a little old lady also grabbed for the same umbrella. She gave Joe the "sad eyes", so Joe quickly stepped back to allow the little old lady to purchase that umbrella.

The street vendor, noticing Joe's act of kindness, offered to sell Joe his one last umbrella that was hidden for himself under the cardboard, street vendor box. Joe was relieved and quickly gave the vendor a $20 bill. The vendor said he had no change. Joe, with only a few dollars left in his bank account, reluctantly said, *"OK, keep the change."*

The street vendor said to Joe, *"THANK YOU VERY MUCH and have a nice day!"* Then the vendor jumped onto a passing bus.

Joe opened the umbrella, but the metal rod was broken and the fabric was ripped. Looking at his watch, now 8:44am, he had only sixteen minutes left to arrive on time for his interview. He looked around, grabbed the street vendor's cardboard box that was left behind and held it up over his head to protect himself from the rain.

As Joe ran down the street with this make-shift, cardboard umbrella, a passing truck hit a deep pothole puddle and splashed muddy water all over him. Joe was now soaking wet from head to toe.

Still determined, he persisted to be on time for his appointment, but frustration filled his face. He looked down at his watch and it was now 8:46am.

Joe finally made it to the interview destination. He entered and headed straight for the elevators. All the elevators were up on the 40th floor. After a full ten minutes of waiting, one elevator car finally made it down to the lobby. Time check: 8:56am

Unfortunately, a mother and her child also entered the elevator. The kid, left unsupervised, decided to hit ALL the floor buttons. Joe's meeting was on the 39th floor. One by one, the elevator stopped at every floor between 1 and 39. Finally, the elevator arrived at floor #39. The digital elevator made its automated voice announcement: *"39th floor, Have a nice day!"*

It's now 9:01am and Joe is late.

He looked around and found the correct office door. It led to the *"Grin and Barrett"* engraving company. Joe entered and saw twenty other male interview applicants seated in that small reception area, all looking neat and clean in their three-piece Armani suits, all holding their individual resume envelopes, all neatly groomed, happy and composed. Joe was soaking wet, with mud-covered pants. The receptionist added Joe's name to the bottom of the list. Joe, still smiling, just leaned against a wall.

Finally, at 11:00am, the receptionist called his name and Joe was directed into the interview room. The interviewer's office chair was turned so Joe could not see the interviewer. He could only see the back of a woman's head. He heard her read his name:

"So, Mr. Smolevecky, tell me about yourself." As she turned and spun her chair to face Joe, it was the little old lady Joe kindly let purchase the street vendor's last umbrella. She looked at Joe. Joe looked at her. She smiled, quickly glanced over Joe's resume, then immediately congratulated him and told him he got the job, and he could start right away. She instructed Joe to go down the hall, make a right and proceed to the engraving room and ask for Ernie the Engraver. Ernie immediately sat Joe down at an engraving machine, gave him a stack of blank, brass signs and showed Joe how to feed those little blank plates into the machine.

One by one, Joe learned how to engrave those signs, and what do you think those little signs read? ... "HAVE A NICE DAY!"

A Gift of Love & Laughter

"HAVE A NICE DAY!"

The following stories are about L♥VE

LIVE, LOVE, LAUGH

LOVE QUOTES

"Love is friendship that has caught fire."
ANN LANDERS

*"Where there is great love,
there are always great miracles."*
MOTHER TERESA

*"I love you not only for what you are,
but for what I am when I am with you."*
ELIZABETH BARRET BROWNING

"The best thing to hold onto in life is each other."
AUDREY HEPBURN

*"Maybe I don't know that much,
but I know this much is true,
I am blessed because I am loved by you."*
UNKNOWN

*"You don't love someone because they're perfect,
you love them in spite of the fact that they're not."*
JODI PICOULT

"Love is an endless act of forgiveness."
PETER USTINOV

*"Being deeply loved by someone gives you strength,
while loving someone deeply gives you courage."*
LAO TZU

TRUE LOVE IS

Couples married fifty years or more
were asked to define TRUE LOVE.
Here are some of their responses:

True love ... is unconditional

True love ... is unwavering

True love ... is unbreakable

True love ... is forever

True love ... is full acceptance of your partner

True love ... is unparalleled devotion for one another

True love ... runs immeasurably deep,
where life without your partner would be unthinkable

True love ... is always using the word "we"
instead of the word "me"

True love ... is being able to totally be yourself
with your partner

True love... dissolves boundaries and separation

True love ... is the trophy in the game of life

I'D CHOOSE YOU

I'd choose you.

In a hundred lifetimes,

in a hundred worlds,

in any version of reality,

I'd find you

and I'd choose you!

"The HEART of a CLOWN"

A Gift of Love & Laughter

EQUATIONS OF L♥VE

ME + U = ♥

TrUe ♥

I am ♥'d
+ U r ♥'d
= We r ♥'d

Give ♥ = Get ♥

My ♥ is yOURS

I ♥ U
+U ♥ Me
♥

All u need is ♥

1 ♥
+ 1 ♥
= 1 ♥

I ♥ U

HOW SHALL I EXPRESS MY LOVE TO YOU?

Shall I simply tell you I love you?
(I know you love hearing it.)

OR

Shall I simply hold your hand?
(I know you love when I hold your hand.)

OR

Shall I simply give you a gift?
(I know you love receiving gifts.)

OR

Shall I simply spend time together with you?
(I know you love when we are together.)

OR

Shall I simply do something special for you?
(I know you love when I do something special for you.)

So hard to choose. I know you love all these things.

OK, I've decided ... I shall do ALL of them!

ALL I NEED IS YOU

They could try their best to bribe me
with a house with an ocean view,
I could never see more beauty
then when I look at you

They could promise daily sunshine,
perfect warmth a lifetime through,
I would rather be on cloud nine
like when I'm holding you

Copyrights to every love song,
all their lyrics old and new,
there's no better sound that I could hear
then you say, *"I love you"*

Hand me keys to vintage autos,
have me own the color blue,
give me all the world's best gold mines,
all I really need is you

Give me riches of a kingdom,
share all secrets known as true,
deeds to all the ancient castles,
all I really want is you

Don't need more things in my life,
here's my reason, here's the clue,
I am such a wealthy man now
'cause Darling, I've got you!

THE GREATEST THING YOU'LL EVER LEARN

*"The Greatest thing you'll ever learn
is to love someone and be loved in return."*

We LIVED
We LAUGHED
We LOVED

We LIVED
We moved, we breathed, we wanted, we received.
We crawled, we walked, we mumbled, we talked.
We wobbled, we steadied, we balanced, we readied.
We studied, we learned, we worked, we earned.

We LAUGHED
We smiled, we cried, we were truthful, we lied.
We giggled, we chortled, we howled, we cackled.
We gaffawed, we snickered, we tittered, we chuckled.
We roared, we "eeeked", we ha-ha-ed, we shrieked.

We LOVED
We grabbed, we felt, we touched, we held.
We gave, we received, we listened, we believed.
We hoped, we beamed, we pondered, we dreamed.
We caressed, we kissed, we hugged, we reminisced.
We remembered, we forgot, we had each other,
... we had a lot.

And we LIVED ... and we LAUGHED ... and we LOVED!

Lake Bessie, Windermere, Fl

A QUIET PLACE

Somedays, I feel I just need to get away from it all.
Sometimes, I just need a day alone,
and that day was today.
For today, I chose to step away ... away from
the hustle and bustle and work and worry.
A time to rest in a moment of reflection,
a moment that was
still, calm, tranquil and restful,
gentle, soothing, private, and peaceful.
Today, I chose a quiet place ...
I stopped, I sat and I pondered.
I reminisced about where I have been,
and how far I have come.
And I dreamed of what might lie ahead.
However, the echo of loneliness had set in,
and absence did make the heart grow fonder.
A realization that loneliness is emptiness ...
and the thought of how much I truly love
and miss you consumes me.
The craving to bathe in your laughter
and swim in your smile.
For it is not a quiet place, but an empty place.
Grow old along with me, for the best is yet to come.
A simple life. A happy life.

Four-year-old
Annie SEVERINI

LOVE

(Through the eyes of a four-year-old)

How do you know your mommy loves you?
"I know mommy loves me 'cause she comes in my room and hugs me at bedtime and tells me she loves me!"

How do you know your daddy loves you?
"I know daddy loves me 'cause he always smiles when he sees me after he comes home late from work, even when he's very tired from working all day."

How do you know your mommy loves your daddy?
*"I know mommy loves daddy 'cause when mommy makes daddy coffee in the morning...
She takes a sip before giving it to him, just to make sure it tastes good."*

How do you know your older sister loves you?
"Well, I know for sure my older sister loves me 'cause she gives me all her old clothes and has to go out and buy all new ones."

How do you know your older brother loves you?
"I know my older brother loves me 'cause when we go to Burger King, he gives me some of his French fries and doesn't even ask me for any of mine."

How do you know your sister and her boyfriend love each other?
"Cause my sister puts on smelly perfume, and her boyfriend puts on stinky shaving stuff, and they go out at night and smell each other."

How do you know when a boy likes a girl?
"Well, you can always tell when a boy likes a girl ... 'cause right after a girl tells a boy she likes his new shirt, he wears it every day."

How do you know your puppy dog loves you?
"Well, I know my puppy dog loves me 'cause he licks my face even after I left him alone all day."

How do you know your grandpa loves your grandma?
"Well, my grandma gots the arthritis and she can't bend over anymore to paint her toenails. I know my grandpa loves nana 'cause my grandpa always bends over and paints nana's toenails for her, even though he gots the arthritis too!"

A Gift of Love & Laughter

TO ALL THE CHILDREN OF THE WORLD

... I WISH YOU ...

Joy ... Health ... Happiness ... Smiles ... Laughter ... Rainbows ... Sunlight ... Beauty ... Strength ... Balance ... Truth ... Faith ... Hope ... Hugs ... Music ... Appreciation ... Comfort ... Peace ...Success ... Friendships ... Excitement ... Pride ... Memories ... Wonderment ... Intelligence ... Honesty ... Respect ... Dignity ... Creativity ... Integrity ... Innocence ... Pleasure ... and Colorful Rainbows ... and LOVE ...
LOTS and LOTS and LOTS of LOVE
ALL the LOVE your heart can hold!

GODSPEED

"I LOVE MY DADDY"
Drawing by
ANNIE SEVERINI

AN OLD IRISH BLESSING

"May you live a long life

Filled with gladness and health,

With a pocket full of gold

As the least of your wealth,

May the dreams you hold dearest,

Be those which come true,

And may the kindness you spread

Keep returning to you!"

UNKNOWN

KID TOYS

"Be the first kid on your block to own one!"

I have always marveled at the advertising slogans created by the Madison Avenue advertising executives, trying to entice a child to empty their piggy bank, deplete their allowance jar or clamor for their parents to withdraw their bank account savings so they could purchase a specific new toy to make the child happy.

There was constant bombardment of TV commercials that repetitively showed an ecstatically happy child playing with the latest toy craze item. Some toys needed a ton of advertising dollars invested to propel their sales into huge profitability, and some toys simply sold themselves. A kid could always look at a toy and know instantly if it piqued their curiosity or tickled their imagination. They all knew if they had to have one; and certainly, many of them wanted to be ... *"the first kid on the block to own one!"*

There were thousands of toys invented - some were fads. Some withstood the test of time. Some still sell heftily today.

I've always loved toys and have always been intrigued by them. I've also always been curious to know why some toys made it big and were kept for years as a childhood memento, and why other toys lost their luster, and eventually were found for sale on the twenty-five cents garage sale pile.

I grew up in a candy store during the middle of the twentieth century, just across the river from NYC. We sold penny candy, homemade lemon ice, packs of baseball cards, and ten cent bottles of Coca Cola. We also sold toys - lots and lots of toys. Our store was located across the street from an elementary school, close to the junior high school, and only a few blocks from the High School. ALL the five-year-old to eighteen-year-old kids in the neighborhood stopped and shopped in our store.

I had the experience of seeing some of these toys when they were first delivered to our store, even before they were advertised, way before they became iconic. Case in point ... My father was friends with one of the *toy jobbers* from NYC. That jobber delivered some of these toys to our store as a test to see how well the toys would sell. Back in 1959, I remember our store receiving the first box of hula hoops. I was ten years old. I tried them out. I couldn't put that hula hoop down. I knew it was going to be a huge hit. We also received some of the first boxes of BARBIE dolls. In addition to selling hula hoops and Barbie dolls, we sold yo-yo's, frisbee's, paddle balls and Slinkys.

So, why did some of these toys "sell like hot cakes" while others were returned back to the manufacturer for a refund? I soon learned that the toys that had an appeal for both a boy or a girl sold the best.

The advertising sales pitches may have resulted in the toy being purchased, but in the end, there was something special and unique about a toy that intrigued or excited the imagination of a child.

Let's take a look ...

What was it about the SLINKY that made millions of kids want one? Was it the fact that each kid could put that Slinky between both of their hands and watch themselves push it back and forth? Was it because each kid controlled it, could command it to walk downstairs as if it had a life of its own? Remarkably, it did. It listened to you and systematically walked down the stairs. I don't really know why a kid wanted to watch a Slinky go down the stairs over and over again, but they did.

Next, the Yo-Yo. It is said that the earliest of yo-yo's dated back to Greece in 500 B.C. Originally, they were made out of clay. Again, a kid could control a Yo-Yo and the more a kid played with their Yo-Yo, the more tricks they learned and the better they could control it.

Let's review some of the top selling toys of the twentieth century and see how a child could control, and enjoy the following toys by using their imaginations as well as their ...

HANDS to control a Slinky or a Yo-Yo.

BALANCE to control a Hula Hoop, POGO STICK, ROLLER SKATES or BICYCLE.

MIND to control and figure out a RUBEX CUBE.

IMAGINATION to control and play with a Barbie Doll (for the girls) or GI Joe Doll (for the boys.)

CREATIVITY to control SILLY PUTTY, PLAY DOUGH or Mr. POTATO HEAD.

OWNERSHIP to play with a CABBAGE PATCH BABY or PET ROCK.

DESIGN TALENTS to control an ERECTOR SET, LINCOLN LOGS or LEGO'S.

Toys ignite a child's creativity by helping them with problem solving issues as well as helping them to develop their motor skills. It never ceases to amaze me when watching the wonderment of a child at play. Sometimes it didn't necessarily even need to be a specific toy. Sometimes it could just be a cardboard box that a kid could make into a fort.

I remember once when my son was about three, I purchased a nice Mickey Mouse toy statue for him. I carefully wrapped it so it wouldn't break and gave it to him for Christmas. He tore off the ribbon, tore off the gift paper, tore open the box, and then said, "WOW, great dad … this is great … BUBBLE WRAP!" … and he played with that bubble wrap for the rest of the day.

PLAY BALL

There is an assortment of various sized, spherical objects which people refer to as a *"BALL."*

"BALLS" are used for play or sport, by males and females who range in age *from 1 to 101.* In many cases, *"BALLS"* are used in various *"BALL"* games where the object of the game has the participant hitting, kicking, throwing, rolling or following the *"BALL"*. Most *"BALL"* games have the player or team of players earning points, and the player or team amassing the greatest number of points wins the *"BALL"* game.

Some *"BALLS"* have traditionally been made of wood, while others were made with a cloth stuffed with rags or horsehair. Some were made from a stitched envelope of leather. In more contemporary times, *"BALLS"* are made from plastic or molded rubber. You can play *"BALL"* games on the ground, in the air, in the grass, on the water, on a smooth, long, slick table, on horseback and on a slate table covered with felt. There's even *"BALL"* games played on a long wooden floor. You can hit, strike, roll or push a *"BALL"* with a wooden stick, with a metal club or with a special paddle. You can also play *"BALL"* games with your hands, feet, head, elbow, neck, shoulder, or ankle. You can play a *"BALL"* game where the object is to hit a *"BALL"* into a cup in the ground, toss a *"BALL"* into a basket on a pole, roll a ball to knock down ten pins, hit a *"BALL"* over a net or fence, and even hit a *"BALL"* into a leather pocket. You can play certain *"BALL"* games by yourself, against one opponent, or play a "BALL" game with one team of players competing against another team of players.

There are specific *"BALLS"* for specific "*BALL* GAMES":

BASEBALL, BASKETBALL, PADDLE BALL, PICKLE BALL, HAND BALL, FOOT BALL, GOLF BALL, POOL BALL, HARD BALL, SOFT BALL, BOCCI BALL, BOWLING BALL, SQUASH BALL, STICK BALL, TENNIS BALL, VOLLEYBALL, WHIFFLE BALL, LACROSS BALL, SOCCER BALL, PING PONG BALL ... And don't forget your MARBLES!

No matter what size, shape, color or weight a *"BALL"* might be, consider that the goal of life is to have a "BALL," and the purpose of a *"BALL"* is a way to have fun.

"Life is like a ball. The deeper we fall, the higher we bounce!"

MAKE A PURE WISH

Close your eyes. Think of something wonderful.
(Your PURE wish can be for you or for someone else.)

A Gift of Love & Laughter

For all the times you might have:

"BLOWN OUT THE CANDLES ON YOUR BIRTHDAY CAKE"

"WISHED UPON A SHOOTING STAR"

"WISHED UPON A RAINBOW"

"FOUND A FOUR-LEAF CLOVER"

"HELD THE BIGGER PART OF THE TURKEY WISH BONE"

"BLEW ON A DANDELION"

"WISHED UPON A LADY BUG"

CONGRATULATIONS

YOUR WISH HAS BEEN GRANTED

INSPIRATION

A BRIDGE TO CROSS
Bridge over Spring Lake, Spring Lake, NJ
(My favorite trout fishing lake in America)

Amazing!

Fabulous!

Wonderful!

Beautiful!

Exceptional!

Absolutely!

Definitely!

Fantastic!

Marvelous!

Brilliant!

Excellent!

Exciting!

Terrific!

Fascinating!

Awesome!

Unbelievable!

I Love it!

FRIENDSHIP

I once had to go into the hospital for some much-needed, serious health-testing. I was scheduled for 5:00am the next morning. The doctor said that I would probably be in the hospital for a day but be prepared to stay a couple of additional days if needed. I was nervous. The hospital was 150 miles away, and I was not allowed to drive myself back home after the tests.

Who could help me?

I immediately thought of three friends that I hoped could possibly come and help me. I instantly knew in my heart that these were three, TRUE FRIENDS of mine.

I called them, one by one but had to leave voice mail messages. All three immediately called me back and said they would drop everything and be there for me one hundred per cent. I know that all three of them knew in their hearts that I would have also dropped everything for them as well. That's what TRUE FRIENDS do.

My anxiety lifted. I felt comforted. I knew I was now in good hands. Everything worked out fine. (Real friends ... "TRUE FRIENDS" are a treasure.)

I was a very rich man that day.

I hope that everyone reading this also has a few wonderful friends they can count on. If you do, you are also a very rich person.

From the hit classic movie: "It's a WONDERFUL LIFE"

> *Dear George: —*
> *Remember <u>no</u> man is a failure who has friends.*
> *Thanks for the wings!*
> *Love*
> *Clarence*

Here are some uplifting quotes I gathered regarding friends and friendship that I hope you will find heart-warming:

"A single rose can be my garden...
a single friend, my world."
— Leo Buscaglia

"Don't walk behind me; I may not lead.
Don't walk in front of me; I may not follow.
Just walk beside me and be my friend."
— Albert Camus

"Best friends understand when you say, 'forget it.'
Wait forever when you say, 'just a minute.'
Stay when you say, 'leave me alone.'
And open the door before you can say, 'come in.'"
— Unknown

*"A friend is someone who understands your past,
believes in your future,
and accepts you just the way you are."*
— **Unknown**

*"Throughout life you will meet one person
who is like no other.
You could talk to this person for hours
and never get bored,
you could tell this person things and
they will never judge you.
This person is your soulmate, your best friend.
Don't ever let them go."*
— **Unknown**

*"True friends are never apart,
maybe in distance but never in heart."*
— **Helen Keller**

*"Sometimes being with your best friend
is all the therapy you need."*
— **Unknown**

A Gift of Love & Laughter

BEFORE

BELIEVE ... before you pray

LISTEN ... before you speak

EARN ... before you spend

THINK ... before you write

TRY ... before you quit

LIVE ... before you die

and

SPEL CHEK ... before you go to print!

CHOOSE

When I was a young boy, it was explained, that as I grew older, I would find that there would be many choices to make in my life ... I was counseled that each choice I made, would carve out the type of person I would become.
I was told to choose wisely.
I was told to ...

CHOOSE what the most important priorities
are in my life

CHOOSE to be happy and have fun

CHOOSE to welcome each new day of life

CHOOSE to live in this moment

CHOOSE to be honest

CHOOSE to have integrity

CHOOSE to have a good positive attitude

CHOOSE to be the best you can be

CHOOSE to always do the right thing

CHOOSE to surround yourself with positive people

CHOOSE to take care of your body and your mind

CHOOSE to smile as much as possible

CHOOSE to help others when you are able

CHOOSE to let go when you know you should let go

CHOOSE to focus on what you already have and
do not worry about what you don't have

CHOOSE to CHOOSE

And remember ...

"To NOT make a choice ... is to make a decision."

"IT'S YOUR ROAD"

"IT'S YOUR ROAD"

It's your road,

and yours

alone.

Other's

may

walk

it

with you,

but

no one

can

walk it

for

you.

MOMENTS FOR ME

I SHALL ...

DANCE ... like nobody's watching
LAUGH ... like everything's funny
SING ... like nobody's listening
WORK ... like I don't need the money

PLAY ... in the sand and the dirt
GIVE ... for all that I'm worth
LOVE ... like I've never been hurt
LIVE ... like it's Heaven on earth

DESTINY

Your BELIEFS become your thoughts,

Your THOUGHTS become your words,

Your WORDS become your actions,

Your ACTIONS become your habits,

Your HABITS become your values,

Your VALUES become your destiny.

MAHATMA GANDHI

BALANCE

"Life is like riding a bicycle.
To keep your balance, you must keep moving."
ALBERT EINSTEIN

FORGIVENESS

(As once told to me by a very wise, little old man.)

*"Never does our human soul become so strong
as when we forgive those that have done us wrong."*

When we forgive ... we do not change the past,
but we do change the future.

Holding on to anger gives you
tense muscles and headaches.

Forgiveness can return laughter back into your life.

Forgiveness ... means to release.

Forgiveness ... is a gift you give to yourself.

Forgiveness ... is choosing to let go of the hurt
and the anger and the temptation to seek revenge.

Forgiveness is choosing healing instead of bitterness.

Forgiveness ... is setting a prisoner free,
then discovering the prisoner was you.

Forgiveness ... is especially important within families.
Sometimes, there can be many family secrets that need to be
healed. For the most part ... most every family has them.
When your anger turns the corner into understanding,

and you begin to feel sorrow for those that have harmed you,
and you no longer have anything left to say,
that's the moment when forgiveness begins.

The Ignorant ... do not forgive nor forget.
The Naïve ... forgive and forget.
The Wise ... forgive but never forget.

You can start right now.

You can stand up for yourself and say ...

"I understand it.

I am finished with it.

I forgive it, but I shall never forget it.

Right this very moment, I forgive myself,

and I set myself free from all that hurt, forever."

WORDS OF WISDOM

(From a Grandfather to a Grandson)

"Throughout my life, I have always felt that a fight has been going on inside my head," said the grandfather to his grandson.

"It's a terrible fight. It's really a fight between a Devil and an Angel."

"The Devil whispers into my left ear. The Devil is evil – he is filled with anger, envy, sorrow, regret, greed, arrogance, self-pity, guilt, resentment, inferiority, lies, false pride, superiority, and ego."

He continued ...

"The Angel whispers into my right ear. The Angel is good – he is joy, peace, love, hope, serenity, humility, kindness, benevolence, empathy, generosity, truth, compassion, and faith."

"The same fight is going on inside of you – and inside every other person as well."

The grandson thought about it for a minute and then asked his grandfather:

"Which one will win?"

The grandfather simply replied:

"The one you listen to the most."

SHIFTING

One of the most difficult lessons in life to learn is to let go
and change how you feel, think, or see things.

Whether it's ...
Guilt, Anger, Love, Loss, Hurt, Grieving or Betrayal,
it's sometimes very hard to change.

Change is never easy.

Sometimes we fight to hold on.
Sometimes we fight to let go.

A wonderfully, wise, and worldly woman once offered
these "words of wisdom" on how she handles change:

*"Though I find it hard to totally let go and totally change,
I do find it easier to think of change in terms of SHIFTING.
Shift a little.
Shift slowly.
Just SHIFT from one gear ... into the next gear.
Slowly let your mind SHIFT into a new way of thinking and
feeling.
Just let it happen.
It happens to work for me.
Maybe it can happen to work for you."*

Remember ... SHIFT HAPPENS!

HAPPY ME

(Lyrics to a song ... with a very catchy beat.)

HAPPY ME, I'm a HAPPY ME,
I will always be, so carefree,
I'm a HAPPY ME

HAPPY HANDS, I've got HAPPY HANDS,
I can lead a band, or make a fan
with my HAPPY HANDS

HAPPY FEET, I've got HAPPY FEET,
they dance to a beat, of a sound so sweet,
I've got HAPPY FEET

HAPPY HIPS, I've got HAPPY HIPS,
they can make me dip, I am such a pip
with my HAPPY HIPS

HAPPY ARMS, I've got HAPPY ARMS,
they add to my charm, and they keep me warm,
My HAPPY ARMS

HAPPY HAIR, I've got HAPPY HAIR,
it flows in the air, makes me debonair,
I've got HAPPY HAIR

HAPPY HEART, I've got a HAPPY HEART,
had it from the start, I would never part
with my HAPPY HEART

HAPPY SMILE, I've got a HAPPY SMILE,
it goes on for miles, just like a child's,
I've got a HAPPY SMILE

HAPPY EYES, I've got HAPPY EYES,
they can tell no lies, make me look wise,
I've got HAPPY EYES

HAPPY ME, I'm a HAPPY ME,
I will always be, so carefree,
I'm a HAPPY ME

MY FAVORITE CLASSIC STORIES ARE STORED IN:
"THE VAULT"

I'm letting a few out. Hope you enjoy them.

A Gift of Love & Laughter

THE PRETZEL LADY AND THE STOCKBROKER

Every day of the work week, Monday through Friday, little old "Sadie the Pretzel Lady" would set up her pretzel stand and sell her homemade pretzels on the New York City Street corner of Wall Street & Exchange Place for twenty-five cents a pretzel.

Every day of the work week, Monday through Friday, Walt, a young stockbroker, would leave his office building at lunch time and as he passed Sadie's little pretzel stand, he would leave Sadie a quarter. But he would never take a pretzel.

This ritual went on for five years, and for those five years, neither of them ever spoke a word to each other.

Finally, one day, as Walt passed Sadie's pretzel stand and left his quarter, Sadie finally broke her silence and spoke to Walt.

Without blinking an eye, Sadie said: *"Hey, they're now thirty-five cents!"*

A Gift of Love & Laughter

The OLD LADY PRETZEL SELLER

(Found this old photo at an antique store in NYC.
Reminds me of when we used to sell pretzels in our family
store for five cents each back in the 1950's.)

THE GOLDFISH BOWL

A high school teacher stood in front of her class and proceeded to present a theory.

She picked up a large, empty, goldfish bowl and proceeded to fill it to the top with ping pong balls.

She asked her students: *"Is the bowl full?"*

Her students all agreed it was full.

The teacher told her students that they were totally incorrect.

She then picked up a box of small, white beans and poured them to the top rim of the bowl.

She shook the bowl lightly, causing the beans to roll into the open areas between the ping pong balls.

Again, she asked her students: *"Is the bowl full now?"*

The entire class agreed that the bowl was full.

"NO", she said. *"You are incorrect."*

Next, she picked up a pail of white, beach sand and carefully poured it into the bowl.

The sand filled all the open space inside the bowl.

The teacher asked the question, *"Is the bowl full now?"*

Apprehensively, the classroom of students pondered a bit, and several students answered that they now felt the bowl was absolutely full.

"Incorrect again" she stated!

Next, she grabbed two large cups of coffee hidden under the table and poured both into the bowl, filling in all the remaining empty space between the sand, the beans, and the ping pong balls so that the liquid of the coffee was completely filled to the brim of the goldfish bowl.

The entire class chuckled.

She let them all think about this for a moment, then she spoke...

"Now, I want you to consider that this goldfish bowl represents your life."

She paused. She gave her students a moment to comprehend that statement. Then she continued ...

"The ping pong balls are the most important things in your life – your family, your children, your health, your friends ... if everything else was gone forever, only your most important things would remain, and your life would still be full.

The beans are the other things that matter to you ... like your job, your house, your car, etc.

The sand is everything else in your life ... the small stuff. If you put the sand into the bowl first, there would be no room for the beans or the ping pong balls.

The same goes for life. If you spend all your time and energy on the small stuff, you will never have room for the important things. So, learn to first pay attention to the most important things in your life that are critical to your happiness.

Take care of your health. Spend time with your family and friends. There will always be time to wash the car, watch TV, play on the computer, etc. Take care of the ping pong balls first – Those are the things that matter most. Know and set all your personal priorities in order. The rest is just sand."

One of the students raised his hand and asked what the coffee represented.

She smiled. *"I'm glad you asked. It just goes to show that no matter how full your life may seem, there's always room for a cup of coffee with a friend."*

YOUR SMILE

*Your SMILE
is your LOGO.*

*Your PERSONALITY
is your BUSINESS CARD.*

*The way you make other's FEEL
is your TRADEMARK.*

FRECKLES

A grandmother took her little granddaughter to the circus. While walking through the lobby on the way to their seats, the grandmother noticed a make-up booth, where a clown was painting kid's faces. Some kids were made up to look like a lion, a tiger, a giraffe or even a clown. The grandmother brought her little granddaughter over to the booth. The little girl wanted to have her face painted as a clown. They stood in line and waited patiently. After waiting a bit, it was finally the little girl's turn.

When the clown looked at the little girl's face, a bratty kid behind her started to make fun of the little girl because she had so many freckles. The bratty kid said: *"Hey Clownie, you're gonna have to use a lot of make-up to cover up all those stupid freckles on that little girl's face."*

The little girl got so embarrassed she actually started to cry. Her grandmother got down on one knee and knelt beside her and said, *"don't listen to that little loudmouth, I love your freckles."*

"Well, I don't like them at all." The little girl replied.

"Oh, honey, when I was a little girl, I always wanted freckles. I think freckles are beautiful!"

The little girl looked up at her grandmother and said, *"Really?"*

A Gift of Love & Laughter

"Of course," said the grandmother. *"Name me one thing that's prettier than freckles."*

The little girl started to dry her tears. She looked up at her grandmother's smiling face, thought about it for a second and answered, *"Well I think that wrinkles are even prettier than freckles."*

Ron applying clown make up on this little freckle-faced girl at Ringling Bros and Barnum & Bailey CIRCUS WORLD.

(Circa 1980)

A GOLF STORY

A priest, a doctor, a rich businessman and a tough guy from NY were waiting one morning for a particularly slow group of golfers in front of them.

The tough guy from NY fumed, *"What's with those jerks? We must have been waiting for forty-five minutes!"*

The doctor chimed in, *"I don't know, but I've never seen such poor golf!"*

The businessman called out *"Move it, time is money"*

The priest said, *"Here comes George the greens keeper. Let's have a word with him."*

"Hello, George!" said the priest. *"What's wrong with that group ahead of us? They're rather slow, aren't they?"*

George the greens keeper replied, *"Oh, yes. That's a group of blind fire fighters. They lost their sight saving our clubhouse from a fire last year, so we always let them play for free anytime."*

The group fell silent for a moment.

The priest said, *"That's so sad. I think I will say a special prayer for them tonight."*

The doctor said, *"Good idea. I'm going to contact my Ophthalmologist colleague and see if there's anything he can do for them."*

The businessman replied, *"I think I'll donate $50,000 to the fire-fighters in honor of these brave souls"*

The tough guy from New York said, *"Why the hell can't they play at night?"*

A SIMPLE LIFE

A wealthy, American businessman decided to vacation by himself in the Bahamas and do some deep-sea fishing. He rented an expensive fishing boat equipped with all top-of-the-line fishing gear. After a full day of fishing, and not even getting one nibble, he decided to reel in his lines and call it a day. He docked his boat directly next to a local, Caribbean fisherman's little fishing boat. This local fisherman had an old torn and repaired fishing net filled with fish. The businessman complimented the fisherman on his abundant catch-of-the-day and asked how long it took him to catch them.

"Not long, just a couple of hours" answered the fisherman.

"But then, why didn't you stay out longer and catch even more?" asked the American.

The fisherman explained that his catch was sufficient to meet his needs and those of his family.

The American asked, *"But what do you do with the rest of your time?"*

"Well, I sleep late, play with my children, and take a siesta with my wife. In the evenings I go into the village to see friends, have a few drinks, play the guitar, and sing a few songs. I have a full but simple life."

The American interrupted, *"I have an MBA from Harvard and a master's in economics, and I can help you!*

"Really?" said the fisherman. *"And what do you suggest that I do?"*

The American proudly explained: *"You should start by fishing longer hours every day so you can catch more fish – this way you can sell the extra fish you catch. With the additional revenue you can buy a bigger boat."*

"And after that?" asked the fisherman.

"With the extra money the larger boat will bring, you can buy a second one, and a third one, and so on until you have an entire fleet of trawlers. Instead of selling your fish to a middleman, you can then negotiate directly with the processing plants and maybe even open your own plant. You can then leave this little island village and move to Miami, or Los Angeles, or even New York City! From there you can direct your huge new enterprise."

"How long would that take?" asked the fisherman.

"Twenty, perhaps twenty-five years," replied the American.

"And after that?"

"Afterwards? Well, my friend, that's when it gets really interesting," answered the American.

"When your business gets really big, you can start buying and selling stocks and make millions!"

"Millions? Really? And after that?" asked the fisherman.

"After that you'll be able to retire, live in a tiny fishing village in the Caribbean, sleep late, play with your children, take a siesta with your wife, and spend your evenings drinking and enjoying your friends ... and live a simple life."

FOR THOSE THAT THINK

For those that think
I should think like them,
please think that through,
then think again!

THE LITTLE BOWL

A little old man went to live with his son, daughter-in-law and five-year old grandson. The old man's hands shook, his eyesight was poor, and he was off balance when he walked. The family all ate together at the table. The elderly grandfather's shaky hands and failing sight made eating difficult. His peas rolled off his spoon and onto the floor. When he grasped the glass, he spilled his milk on the tablecloth. The son and daughter-in-law became very upset with the mess.

"We have to do something about Grandfather," said the son. *"I've had enough of his spilled milk, noisy eating and food on the floor."*

So the husband set a little table in the corner. Their Grandfather ate alone. Since Grandfather had broken a dish or two, his food was now served in a little wooden bowl. When the family glanced in Grandfather's direction, sometimes he had a tear in his eye as he sat alone. Still, the only words the couple had for him were sharp admonitions when he had dropped a fork or spilled food. The five-year-old watched it all in silence.

One evening before supper, the father noticed his five-year old son playing with wood scraps on the floor. He asked the child,

"What are you making?"

The boy responded with great tenderness,

"I'm making a little bowl for you and Mama to eat your food in when I grow up."

The five-year-old smiled and went back to work.

The words so struck the parents that they were speechless. Then tears started to stream down their cheeks. Though no word was spoken, both knew what must be done. That evening the husband took Grandfather's hand and gently led him back to the family table. For the remainder of his days, he ate every meal with the family. And for some reason, neither husband nor wife seemed to care any longer when a fork was dropped, when milk was spilled or when the tablecloth was soiled.

IS IT TRUE?

Is it true ... four nickels equal a Paradigm?

Is it true ... half a large intestine equals One Semicolon?

Is it true ... two thousand pounds of Chinese soup equals Won Ton?

Is it true ... one million pains in your body equals One Megahertz?

Is it true ... one unit of laryngitis equals One Hoarse Power?

Is it true ... one million microphones equal One Megaphone?

Is it true ... 2000 mockingbirds equal Two Kilomockingbirds?

Is it true ... the shortest distance between two jokes equals a Straight Line?

A Gift of Love & Laughter

THIS IS THE END OF

"THE VAULT STORIES"

NOW COME

"THE DRAWINGS"

"THE CHARTS"

*"So, which chart is my blood pressure ...
And which chart is the stock market:"*

A Gift of Love & Laughter

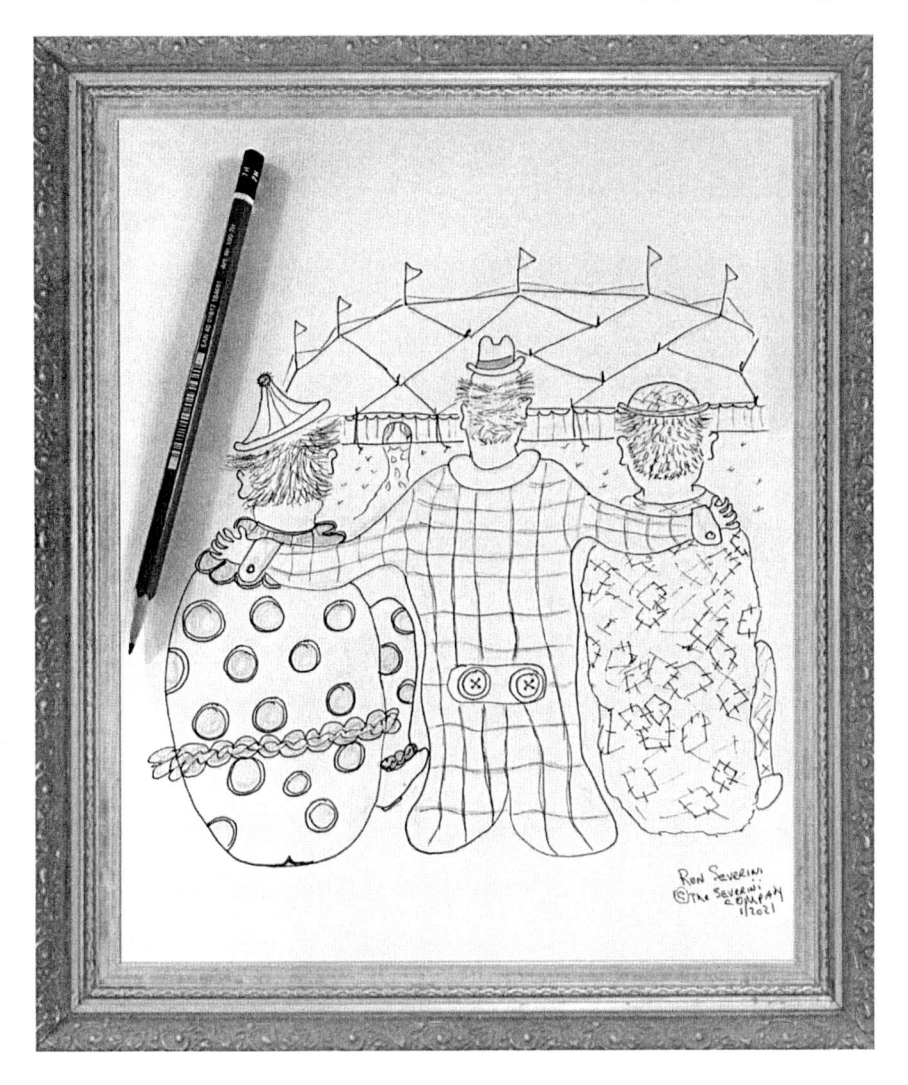

"BOBBY, LOU, OTTO"

(Bobby Kay, Lou Jacobs, Otto Griebling ... three of the greatest Ringling Bros and Barnum & Bailey Circus Clowns of the Twentieth Century.)

"HAIR TODAY ... GONE TOMORROW!"

*"Yeah, now our hair just grows
in our nose and ears where we don't need it!"*

A Gift of Love & Laughter

"The LOONEYVILLE LIBRARY"

New Self-Help Book: *"HOW TO GET A-HEAD"*

My Mentor

OTTO GRIEBLING

(April 28, 1896 – April 19, 1972)

The GREAT American Circus Clown

A Gift of Love & Laughter

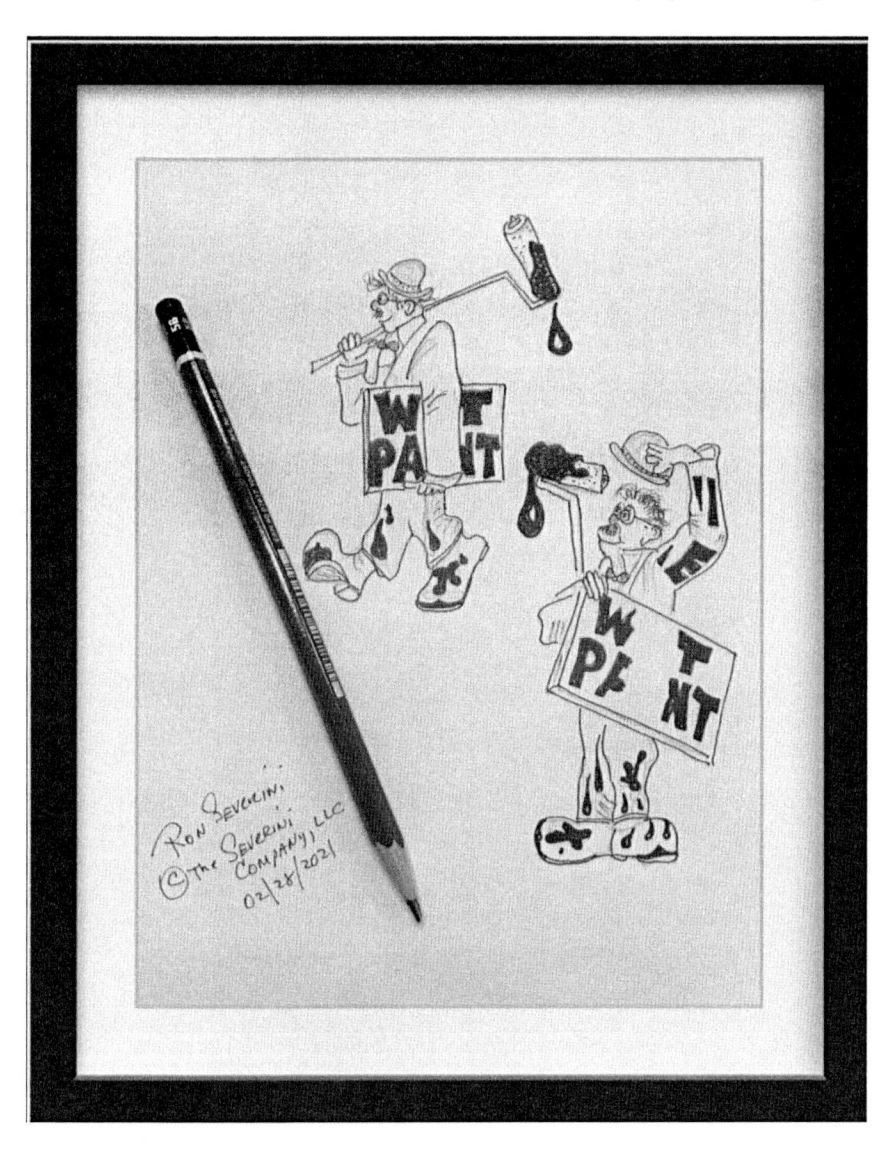

"WET PAINT"

146

"The ARTIST"

ART ... is in the eye of the beholder.

A Gift of Love & Laughter

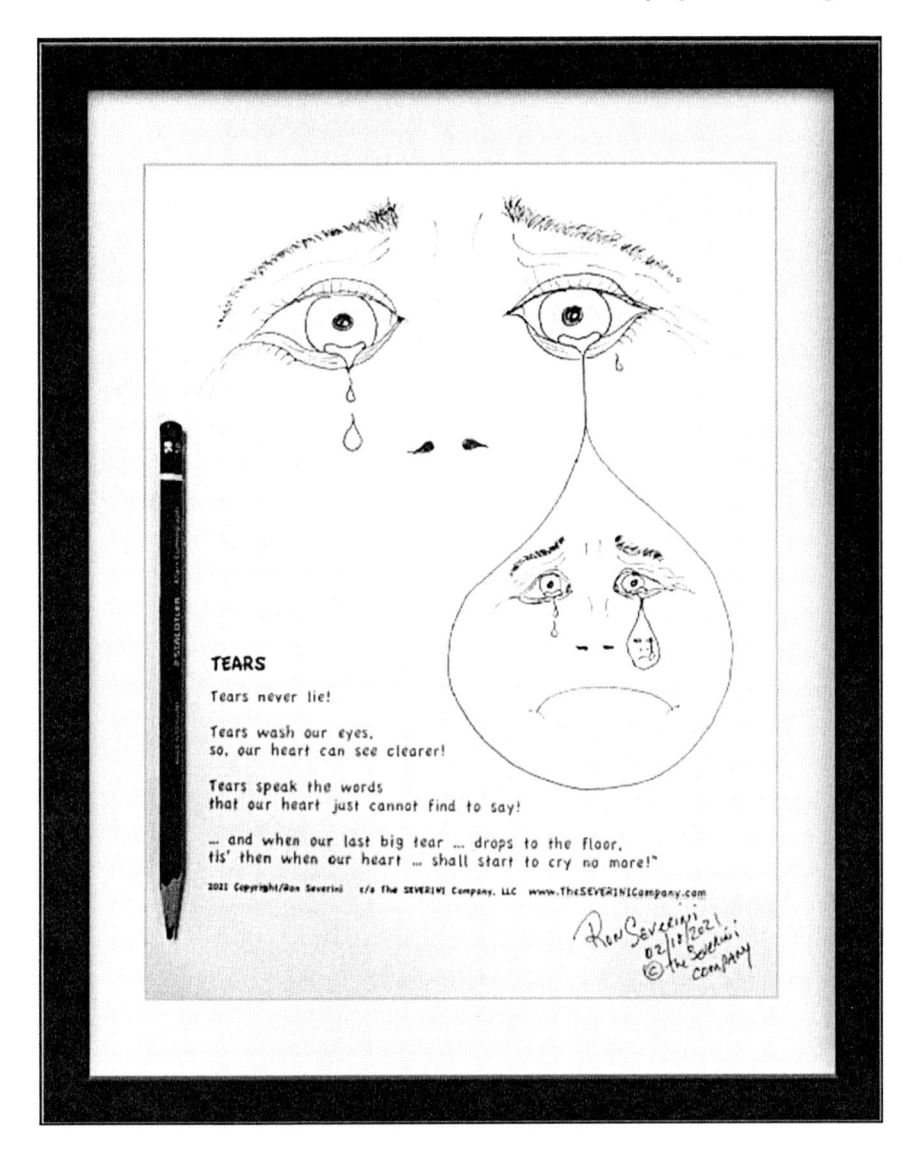

"TEARS"

Tears ... never lie!
TEARS ... wash our eyes so our hearts can see clearer.
TEARS ... speak the words our hearts cannot find to say.
And when our last big TEAR drops to the floor,
'tis then our heart shall cry no more!"

AND NOW ...

A FEW MORE
"SILLY STORIES"

A Gift of Love & Laughter

STORIES COURTESY OF THIS CENTURY OLD UNDERWOOD TYPEWRITER

"TOMMY The TURKEY BOY"

A Gift of Love & Laughter

TOMMY THE TURKEY BOY

After hiding reclusively in his mobile home for 364 days, (Tommy never goes out and he especially always stays indoors on Thanksgiving)... retired side-show performer, *"Tommy, The Turkey Boy"* will finally be going outside of his house to walk around his neighborhood of Gibsonton, FL to celebrate Halloween.

Halloween is the only day of the year that Tommy feels comfortable in venturing out. I know you will ALL wish Tommy well on his walk around the neighborhood.

"Break a Drumstick, Tommy!"

LOONEY LARRY

I have a very dear friend by the name of "Looney Larry". Larry used to suffer from depression, but he doesn't suffer from depression anymore. Miraculously, "Looney Larry" found himself a cure. You see, Larry's main cause of depression was the fact that he could never get along with anyone, especially with any of his neighbors. Each time Larry would come in contact with any of the people living close to him, he'd always end up in a big argument, eventually escalating into fist fights. This depressed Larry greatly.

To combat his depression, Larry created a little ritual for himself. Now, this might not cure anyone else, but it certainly worked for Larry. Here's "Looney Larry's" self-prescribed depression remedy. Each time Larry would start feeling depressed, he'd go out in front of his house and stand in the middle of the street, and he'd yell out at the top of his lungs, over and over and over again, a silly little ditty that he wrote:

"I'm alright ... I'm OK ...
I'm not gonna let depression get to me anymore
DEPRESSION is nothing but a DENT
And a DENT is nothing but a HOLE
And a HOLE is nothing but a big fat ZERO
Zilch, Zippo, Nada, Goose Egg, a big fat Zero
And a big fat ZERO is just plain NOTHING
So, if you think I'm gonna stand here and
get depressed over nothing, YOU'RE nuts!"

Then Larry would always spin around, counterclockwise in a circle, three times in a row, and with a great big smile on his face, he'd let out at the top of his lungs, a huge belly laugh, and he'd keep laughing and laughing until he felt better.

And that's how "Looney Larry" cured himself.

It's unfortunate that no one in his neighborhood congratulated "Looney Larry", as just when Larry finally fully cured himself, ... all his neighbors had moved away.

THE QUIRKY CHEMIST

There once was a kooky, crazy, quirky, yet uniquely clever chemist.

He dreamed of inventing amazing creations to help the world (while also making himself rich in the process.)

One of his most brilliant ideas was to invent a liquid that could dissolve anything.

After years of investing his time in experimentation, he finally found the perfect liquid solution.

He tested it over and over and found that it worked perfectly!

He spilled a little on a piece of paper, and low and behold, the paper dissolved!

He brushed a little on a piece of plastic, and again, as if by magic, the plastic completely disappeared!

He kept on testing. He poured a little on a piece of cotton, a piece of wood, a piece of tin, a piece of glass, an old silver dollar, and even on a piece of stainless steel. All of those items completely vanished!

He was thrilled. His experiment worked. He was finally going to be a success!

He was finally on his way to becoming enormously wealthy.

With the money he would receive, he envisioned building a brand-new, state-of-the-art laboratory where he could invent all the things, he had ever dreamed of creating during his lifetime.

His next step ... to set up an appointment to bring his newfound disappearing liquid to the biggest company in America.

He did his research. He made his contact. His meeting was finally set for the following day.

He couldn't wait to show off his miracle mixture.

He got up early the next day, dressed and got ready to drive to his meeting to show off his creation.

However, he found that he had just one more major hurdle yet to overcome.

He couldn't find a package to put it in.

The FISHERMAN and the RABBI

As unbelievable as this story might read, it's 100% true ...

I was fishing one day at my favorite, rainbow trout location in Spring Lake, NJ. After temping trout for over eight hours with a wide selection of worms, corn and salmon eggs, I still hadn't had a nibble. The sun was beginning to set, and I was contemplating packing up for the night. Suddenly, a medium-sized, bearded man, wearing a black hat, black overcoat, white shirt with a black tie walked directly towards me. He stopped about six feet away, and he just stood there for maybe ten minutes, watching and silently studying me fish. Finally, he broke the silence and spoke:

"So, how do you know if you've hooked a fish?"

I listened intently and then answered: *"Well, the line will go shooting straight out and the tip of my fishing pole will bend down towards the water. That's when I'll quickly pull up my rod and try to set the hook in the fish's mouth. Then I will keep the line tight and slowly reel him in as best as I can."*

He then said: *"During my entire life I've never gone fishing."*

I responded: *"Well, would you like me to teach you?"* ... And with that he responded: *"Yes, I would LOVE for you to teach me how to fish."*

Proudly, I quipped ... *"Well, this just might be the day that your life will change forever. Let me introduce myself. My name is Ron, but my close friends call me Ronnie.*

And he said: *"Well, Ronnie, my name is Rabbi Shulman, and you can simply call me Rabbi.*

Then I said: *"Ya know Rabbi, I have always heard the saying that if you give a child a fish, they will have a fish to eat for one day, but if you teach a child to fish, then the child can go fishing any time they want, catch their own fish, and then they will be able to eat fish for the rest of their life. I'm sure it works for Rabbi's just as well."*

And he said: *"A very wise and appropriate saying."*

So ... I proceeded: *"OK Rabbi, first I'll teach you how to put on the bait. To start, take this worm and carefully stick it on the end of this hook."* (Which he did.)

Then I put my fishing rod in his hands and showed him how to cast the line.

But before he had the chance to cast, I stopped him and asked if he would bless the water for good luck.

He did.

After a few fumbling attempts the Rabbi cast the line and did it perfectly. No sooner did that worm hit the water when the line went shooting out. The Rabbi had hooked into one! I told him to pull back on the line, set the hook, then keep the line very tight. I instructed him not to crank the reel too fast, just feel the fish on the line and have fun reeling him in.

He did it.

It was all so surreal to watch the Rabbi reel in his fish. He had the most magical, child-like smile on his bearded face, looking like a little 9-year-old youngster on Rabbi dress-up day, catching a fish for the very first time. However, when he reeled in his fish, the line got wrapped around a rock that was close to the shoreline causing it to snap, and the fish got away.

I said: *"Oh no, Rabbi, what happened? I thought you blessed the lake and everything would be fine!"*

With a solemn, disappointing look on his face that went from one side of his wing-spanned beard to the other, the Rabbi sadly replied: *"Well, I did bless the lake, but I forgot to bless the shore!"*

He handed me back my fishing rod and said he had a wonderful experience, and he'll think about fishing again someday, now that he was taught by such an excellent teacher.

Then he asked: *"And is there anything that I can I teach you, my son"?*

I thought to myself for a moment and then asked him: *"Yeah, do you know any good rabbi jokes? You know, like a priest, a minister and a rabbi go into a bar."*

He looked shocked at my request, but then he thought about it for a couple of long seconds, looked around to see if anyone was listening, then whispered to me: *"YES, YES I DO! did you ever hear the one about the priest, the minister and the rabbi that go fishing?"*

... and he playfully proceeded to tell me this story ...

"A priest, a rabbi and a minister go fishing on a rare day off. They rowed their boat far away from shore and put down an anchor. The boat moved just a little bit here and there. The three of them enjoyed being away from their jobs. The fishing was very relaxing, and they exchanged funny stories about their lives.

The priest said: *'Well, I have to go and use nature's rest room.'* He stepped out of the boat and walked on top of the water to the shore, 'did his thing' and walked on top of the water back to the boat and got back in.

The rabbi was astonished but said nothing. A while later, the minister said: *'Well, I guess it's my turn now.'* He stepped out of the boat, walked on the water to the shore and 'did his thing' and returned to the boat by walking on the water and got back into the boat.

The rabbi was again amazed, saying nothing. When it came time for the rabbi to 'do his thing', he told himself that if they can do it so can he. So, he stepped out of the boat and immediately plunged deep into the water. The priest and the minister helped him back into the boat. They looked at each other, and the minister said: *'Maybe we should have shown the rabbi where the rocks were?"*

His story cracked me up, and I almost fell into the lake myself from laughing so hard ... and with that, Rabbi Shulman's eyes opened wide, his smile filled his face, he let out a huge laugh, turned, chuckled, thanked me for the fishing lesson and walked away into the sunset.

I never saw him again, but I shall always remember my new-found, fishing friend, forever."

This is a very true story ... but if you don't believe it, just stop, and think ... who are you going to believe ... ME or the rabbi?

FICTIONAL CHARACTERS

Growing up, a child is told about some wonderful, magical, fictional characters. Some of these iconic characters are attached to a holiday, while others are associated with an event or a time of season.

CUPID for Valentine's Day
LEPRECHAUN for St Patrick's Day
EASTER BUNNY for Easter
MOTHER EARTH for Earth Day
TOOTH FAIRY for the night a child loses their first tooth
UNCLE SAM for the Fourth of July
JACK O'LANTERN for Halloween
SANDMAN for the night a child can't fall asleep
JACK FROST for Winter
SANTA CLAUS for Christmas
FATHER TIME for New Year's Eve
BABY NEW YEAR for New Year's Day

I shall admit that I believed in all of them, and I still do. And why not? I think you can live a charmed life if you are still a "kid at heart". One of my favorite phrases has always been said at the beginning of every circus performance.
It is when the Ringmaster blows his whistle and says:

"LADIES and GENTLEMEN and "Children of All Ages!"

I believe there's a child in all of us.

A Gift of Love & Laughter

I BELIEVE

"*Yes, I still do believe in Santa Claus!*"

I believe in the power of the thought that there really is a kind, little, old man that gives free toys and gifts to all the children around the world; and that he does this solely on one very special night each year called Christmas.

I believe Santa goes from house to house by soaring through the sky in his mystical sled, pulled by eight flying reindeer, led by one special reindeer, named Rudolph, who has a magical red nose that lights the way.

I believe in kindness.

I believe in giving.

I believe in the wonderment of it all.

I believe in the smell of chestnuts roasting on an open fire, the sound of jingling bells, the majesty of new fallen snow, the sight of lit Christmas lights all aglow down the streets of a small town, and I certainly believe in the power of Mistletoe.

I believe someone is keeping track if I am naughty or nice, and that I will always be rewarded accordingly if I am nice.

I believe Elves do live in the North Pole, and they are capable of making any toy imaginable for Santa to deliver.

I believe that if you wish for a fire truck under the tree on Christmas morning, it just might appear ... it worked for me!

A Gift of Love & Laughter

I believe in the hope within the heart of every child on
Christmas Eve.

I believe in the excitement in the soul of every living person
on Christmas morning.

I believed, that if I wished for a shiny new bicycle,
that it just might have been there under the tree on
Christmas morning.

And it was!

I believe in candy canes and Frosty the Snowman.

I believe in the taste of piping hot chocolate on a cold winter night.

I believe reindeers really can fly, if they want to fly.

I believe that giving feels so much better than receiving.

I believe wonderful things can come in small packages.

I believe that hope is an enormously powerful human force.

I believe dreams really can come true.

Yes, I believe in the magic of the thought

A Gift of Love & Laughter

that there really is a Santa Claus.

I believe in the power of true love.

... and YES, I do believe in Santa Claus,
and I have believed in him ever since my very first Christmas!

May the magic of Santa Claus and the spirit of Christmas
continue to fill your heart for all the days of your life!
Life can be like that EVERY DAY if you want it to be.

BELIEVE

Peace! Love! Health! Happiness!

A FULL GLASS OF LIFE

FULL: *(Adjective; Verb; Adverb)*
Containing or holding as much as possible, leaving no empty space. Not lacking or omitting anything.
Complete.

There has always been a question bantered throughout the ages, asking people how they perceived various aspects of their life. Did they view their "imaginary glass of life" to be half-EMPTY or half-FULL?

In hearing an abundant assortment of colorful responses, it seems as though many people answer from the vantage point that life is best lived if one views life with a glass that is half-full. In other words, to be happy living life for what one does have, as opposed to being unhappy for what one does not have.

It is possible that those people that had absolutely nothing at one time during their life, perceived their "glass of life" to be half-full - in essence, to be "happy to have more than nothing." If one perceives a half-full or a half-empty glass, it is all a subjective matter for each individual.

For me, when I was a child, my mother used to ask if I was FULL, but I knew she was really asking me about my tummy. As I grew a bit older, she would periodically still ask me that same question, but I knew she was really asking a different question. Though she was asking me if I was FULL, she was actually asking if I was happy? If I was content? If I was living a FULL life?"

In thinking about her repeated inquiry, I found myself pausing and asking a string of questions that I felt compelled to answer for myself:

"What is the definition of the word FULL?"

"What does it look like to view my glass as half empty?"

"What does it look like to view my glass as half FULL?"

"What is MY definition of living a FULL life?"

"Is MY definition of living a FULL LIFE the same as other people's definition?"

"Does everyone strive to live a FULL life?"

"How would I feel about myself if I didn't live a FULL life?"

"Do those people that are NOT living a FULL life, have regrets?"

"Would I have regrets if I didn't live a FULL life?"

"Would my definition of the word FULL consistently mean the same throughout my years, or would it evolve throughout my life as I got older?"

As a young man, I remember reading this quote from ALBERT EINSTEIN, which really resonates with me till this day:

"Live Life to the fullest. You have to color outside the lines once in a while if you want to make your life a masterpiece.

Laugh some every day. Keep growing, keep dreaming, keep learning, keep following your heart." - **ALBERT EINSTEIN**

Thus, from that moment of reading Mr. Einstein's quote, I began to research more quotes from some other iconic people throughout history. I ultimately came to value all of their quotes. I found them inspiring. They have helped me to realize what was important in my life. Some of these thoughts I grasped right away, while others had me adjusting my sails for a very long time.

"To live a FULL life, discover and pursue your life's purpose. Strive to discover who you are, what is your life mission, and what you are trying to become. Always be a good person. Always care for your soul."
SOCRATES

"The purpose of life is to live it, to taste life experiences to the utmost, to reach out eagerly and without fear for newer and richer experiences!" **ELEANOR ROOSEVELT**

"Life is short, break the rules. Forgive quickly, kiss slowly. Love truly. Laugh uncontrollably and never regret anything that makes you smile." **MARK TWAIN**

"Life is either a daring adventure or nothing."
HELEN KELLER

"Life is a game, PLAY IT. Life is a challenge, MEET IT. Life is an opportunity. CAPURE IT." **PLATO**

"All life is an experiment. The more experiments you make the better." **RALPH WALDO EMERSON**

"Go confidently in the direction of your dreams. Live the life you have imagined." **HENRY DAVID THOREAU**

"Don't wait for the right opportunity. Create it."
GEORGE BERNARD SHAW

"If you can dream it, you can do it!" **WALT DISNEY**

"Your time is limited, so don't waste it living someone else's life." **STEVE JOBS**

"It's never too late to be what you might have been."
GEORGE ELLIOT

"If you obey all the rules, you'll miss all the fun."
KATHARINE HEPBURN

"Nothing is more precious than being in the present moment. Fully alive, fully aware." **THICH NHAT HANH**

"To live a FULL Life, consider it a great big canvas, and throw all the paint on it you can." **DANNY KAYE**

"Twenty years from now you will be more disappointed by the things you didn't do than by the things you did."
MARK TWAIN

So, I hope you have found these quotations thought-provoking and even inspirational.

May you all have a long and healthy and ***FULL*** life!

FULL

To help you calculate whether you've had a *FULL* LIFE thus far ... and if you perceive it to be Half EMPTY or Half *FULL*, consider directing your *FULL* ATTENTION to this silly little LIST of Forty *FULL* items below. Have you ever had ...

___ A FULL HEAD of Hair

___ A FULL PLATE of Spaghetti

___ A FULL BELLY

___ A FULL TANK of Gas

___ A FULL PHYSICAL

___ A FULL BODY Work Out

___ A FULL-STOCKED Refrigerator

___ A FULL PANTRY of Food

___ Are you FULL of Love

___ FULL of Surprises

___ FULL of Adventures

___ A FULL COUNT in Baseball (3 balls and 2 strikes)

___ Paid FULL ATTENTION

A Gift of Love & Laughter

___ A FULL SWING at Bat

___ Played the FULL GAME

___ Played the FULL SEASON

___ FULL-TIME Employee

___ A FULL GLASS of Water

___ Drinking FULL-BODIED Merlot

___ Sleeping on a FULL-SIZED Mattress

___ A FULL HOUSE (beats a Flush)

___ A FULL MOON

___ FULL AUTO Insurance Coverage

___ Playing with a FULL DECK

___ FULL RETIREMENT

___ FULL HEALTH-CARE Coverage

___ Received a FULL PENSION

___ FULL VIEW

___ FULL COURT Press

___ Coming FULL CIRCLE

___ FULL DISCLOSURE

___ Get the FULL EFFECT

___ BE GIVEN FULL IMMUNITY

___ HAVE A FULL DANCE Card

___ FULL NAME

___ Had A FULL PROOF Plan

___ FULL CONCENTRATION

___ FULL of THEMSELVES

___ FULL of CRAP

___ Are you living a FULL LIFE?

A Gift of Love & Laughter

Is your glass half empty or half full?

BE THANKFUL

I was once told to ...

Be THANKFUL for difficult times ...
those are the times you grow.
So, be THANKFUL

Be THANKFUL for limitations ...
limitations encourage resourcefulness.
So, be THANKFUL

Be THANKFUL for challenges ...
challenges build strength and character.
So, be THANKFUL

Be THANKFUL for ~~misteaks,~~ ...
mistakes help you learn.
So, be THANKFUL

Be THANKFUL for what you have ...
don't focus on what you don't have.
So, be THANKFUL

THANK YOU for reading my book.

I hope you enjoyed it

THANK YOU!

A Gift of Love & Laughter

THANK YOU

Muchas gracias

Molto grazie

Muito obrigado

Merci beaucoup

Danke schön

Dank je wel

Tack så mycket

Þakka þér fyrir

Asante sana

Очень Спасибо

شكرا جزيلا

धन्यवाद

நன்றி

ABOUT THE AUTHOR

RON SEVERINI

*CEO, Executive Producer, Artistic Director, Author
Talent Agent, Talent Casting Director, Talent Manager
Professor, Writer, Professional Circus Clown
Pop-Pop*

The SEVERINI Company, LLC / Windermere, FL *(2016 -)*
CEO / Executive Producer / Artistic Director / Dreamer

CASTLE TALENT, Inc / Orlando, Fl *(2001 - 2015)*
Executive Producer / CEO / Talent Agent

WALT DISNEY COMPANY / Orlando, Fl (1990 - 2000)
Talent Casting & Booking Director

FELD ENTERTAINMENT / Venice, Fl *(1971 - 1990)*
*Professional Clown / Boss Clown / Ambassador of Goodwill
Director* / Ringling Bros. and Barnum & Bailey Clown College
Director of Clowns / Circus World Theme Park / Orlando, Fl
Special Project Manager / Worldwide

ADDITIONAL CREDITS:
Executive Producer / Gazillion Bubble Show / Off Broadway
Talent Agent / Siegfried & Roy Presents
Talent Agent / America's Got Talent
Talent Agent / Cirque du Soleil
Talent Judge / Star Search / CBS TV
Co-Writer / Dick Van Dyke / CBS TV Special

Professor / Lehigh University / Bethlehem, PA
First-ever accredited course in:
"*The Study of the American Clown*"

AUTHOR / Book Titles:

OTTO GRIEBLING / *The Great American Circus Clown*

JIM HOWLE / *The ART of a CLOWN*

RINGLING REMEMBERED ... Through the Eyes of a Clown

A GIFT OF LOVE & LAUGHTER

AWARDS:

DRAMA DESK AWARD / Co-Producer
"*Most Unique Theatrical Experience in America*"
Off Broadway

LIFETIME ACHIEVEMENT AWARD
Legacy of Laughter / World Clown Association

FIRST PLACE - AUTHOR AWARD
World Clown Association

If you enjoyed this book, then you should love:

RINGLING REMEMBERED
"Through the Eyes of a Circus Clown"
Ron Severini, Author

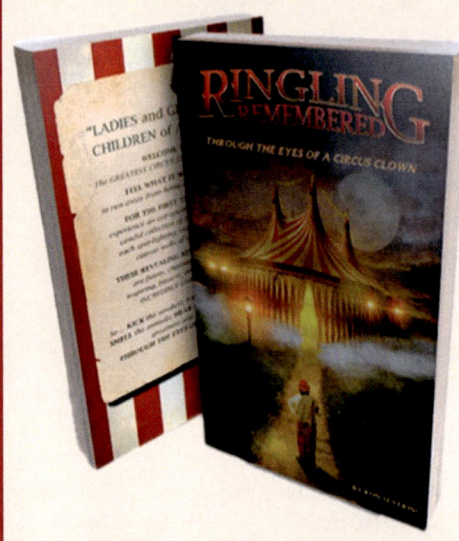

> Ron Severini is a font of circus memories and experiences. His book paints an amazing picture of life spent with The Greatest Show on Earth. Perfect for any history or circus buff!

—PRICILLA MOOSEBURGER,
Director of Mooseburger Clown Arts Camp

> This is a GREAT BOOK! I highly recommend it to all.

—SCOTT O'DONNELL,
Executive Director Circus World/Baraboo

Available in print and Kindle on
AMAZON.COM
TheSEVERINIcompany.com

A Gift of Love & Laughter

HEWETT-WELLINGTON HOTEL
Spring Lake, New Jersey

This book was written within the walls of the Hewitt-Wellington Hotel

It is my favorite Hotel in all of America

Simple, quiet, peaceful, charming, inspiring

It's a *"Home away from home."*

THANK YOU, Mathew, and THANK YOU all for your hospitality.

If you'd like to order a copy of this book for a friend,
please visit us at:
TheSEVERINIcompany.com

If you'd like to be informed of future books,
please contact us at:
Info@TheSEVERINIcompany.com

A Gift of Love & Laughter

"ART IS NEVER FINISHED, ONLY ABANDONED!"
Leonardo Da Vinci

With that quote ... I shall abandon my book.

###